WRITING WITH A DAY JOB

CREATING WHAT YOU WANT WHILE DOING WHAT YOU NEED TO

JAMES BEACH

MIND
FU

WRITING WITH A DAY JOB

This work is designed to provide accurate and authoritative information in regard to the subject matter covered. Neither the author nor the publishers are engaged in rendering legal, accounting or other professional advice. If expert assistance is desired, the services of a competent professional should be sought.

All examples cited in the book are used for illustrative purposes only, and do not constitute professional advice.

A Mind Fu original book. 29 Grove St., #340

San Francisco, CA 94102

ISBN: 978-1-945451-12-6

Cover art direction by James Beach

First printing. January 2020

v1.4

CONTENTS

DEDICATION

To all the artists, everywhere and everywhen:

*Thank you for helping us
feel, explore, understand and evolve
what it means to be human.*

*Thank you for helping
our connection to you,
each other, ourselves, and life.*

*Thank you for your creations
and how they help us be.*

ABOUT THIS BOOK

This book is about overcoming the many unique challenges that come from loving to create, while not yet having your life set up so that you can spend most of your day creating.

It's about finding ways to do what you want, and the defiant success that resourcefulness applied can bring to you and your life.

It's about making it happen until you can make it full time—and enjoying and discovering yourself, and expressing what you find along the way.

To those ends, this book shares strategies and ways of being that have worked for me.

CONTENTS SHIFT ACCORDING **to altitude**

This book is structured to start at a high level and then zoom into the details. In that analogy, this part you're still reading is observing the topics from about 10,000 feet in height. In Part 2 we'll zoom in and observe the overall forest, in Part 3 we'll float down to right above the trees, and in Part 4 we'll get down to the tree level and start checking out the bark.

I am primarily a writer. At the same time, I am also a fine arts photographer and a recovering musician. And I have found in my long time creating that a lot of creative issues are pretty universal to all creative artists.

To that end, the first 3 parts of this book are about concerns that apply to most any artist balancing any creative endeavor with a day job. The 4th part delves into software tools for all art forms, and then some specific tactics for creative writing in particular.

Outside Sources

A fair amount of the information in here comes from leaning over the shoulders of giants and having my own take on it, while I have worked an absurd range of different jobs. I aim to credit the originator of the idea wherever I can recall it. Where I might be wrong or might not have acknowledged someone, I apologize in advance and would love to hear the right information so I can correct it. I also include a list of sources I've found useful at the end.

PG-13 technical terminology

My language may verge into adult phrases i.e. curse words. This fittingly termed "adult language" can be the clearest, most accurate and most appropriate way to refer to some specific kinds of people or situations.

As a plain example, sometimes the clearest and most appropriate terms for difficult people and unfair situations are, respectively, "assholes" and "horseshit".

For some people and situations, this may in fact be a polite understatement.

And my thanks

Thanks so much for reading this. It honors me. May this book provide usefulness for you in doing what you want, as the exploration that led to creating it has provided for me.

My hope is that you will find useful ways of being, attitudes, strategies and tools to create, produce, and create for yourself an atmosphere of resourcefulness to bring your creative dreams to fruition.

While doing what you have to do, making more of what you want to.

OVERALL PRINCIPLES

Before going into making what we want, it's good to delve a bit into our doing what we have to do. Until that point when we don't need day jobs as much, it's important that we have a clear and useful understanding of the territory.

As the great songwriter and musician Bill Withers said, "You know, it's okay to head out for Wonderful. But on your way to Wonderful, you're gonna have to pass through All Right. And when you get to All Right, take a good look around, and get used to it."

So here are the overall principles that operate in all realms, up to All Right and including Wonderful.

You can learn to do almost anything you want.

Yes, you.

It is my firm conviction, backed by own personal experience and my observation of others, that we can learn how to do just about anything we want to do. The details of technique don't need to be a barrier to any form of creative expression. All the artists we love are human. They did amazing things we are grateful for, and in a way they were better than gods: they were born of woman the same as you and me. Some learned easy, like Mozart or Edgar Rice Burroughs. Some learned with great effort, like Stevie Ray Vaughan or Joseph Conrad. All learned.

With this principle in mind, this book focuses less on the technical details of writing or other fields of expression, and more topics I haven't seen put together in other books. Such as ways to approach the emotional management and project management we need to create the work we want, while still doing the other work we have to.

With this principle in mind, this book focuses less on the technical details of writing or other fields of expression, and more topics I haven't seen put together in other books. Such as ways to approach the emotional management and project management we need to create the work we want, while still doing the other work we have to.

Do no harm to yourself

I want this book to be as helpful as possible to anyone taking this on. It will only be natural that some of it won't work for you. I'd say it's even statistically certain, as we're all different people. These kinds of differences are more than fine, they are absolutely as they should be.

So only take from this book what helps you. And if any part of it does not work for you, feel free to junk it.

I also invite you to try things on as a test. Set a certain amount of time and see what the results are, and how you feel about them. Just explore some methods that are new from any other angle you like, and see if they hold some value or utility for you. And if it turns out they don't, there's no need to try them any further.

A good way to look at this is practice and training for developing *your own* systems that work for you. Which you can even write your own book about.

This is offered in the spirit of joy and fun, and grabbing as much creative production as we can with both hands and feet. Getting to know what works for us helps us to know and care for ourselves. And testing those boundaries by mixing in new possible actions and ways healthily expands our comfort zones. Expanding a comfort zone can't help but mean some discomfort - much like physical exercise. And also like physical exercise, it is good for us.

We will find more things that we find comfortable and even that we enjoy.

No matter what, this is all in the clear context of you doing whatever you want to as a human being. You are the ultimate and rightful captain of you.

THE POWER **of art**

Art matters. And more specifically, *your* art matters. Every person in the world, no matter how macho or tough or "realistic" they think they are, has at least one bit of art that brings a tear to their eye or a smile to their face. Or both within the span of an instant. Something that has deep meaning for them and gives beauty to their lives. It could be a song, a movie, a story, a painting, a joke. Whatever it is, it reached across the boundaries that are often between us to touch something deep inside them.

Artistic creation, among many other things, provides enriching human experiences that nothing else can provide. Something that strikes deep chords within us, bringing has deep meaning and beauty to our lives.

If at the end of the day your heart makes only one person smile, even if that one person is you, then you have won.

And we want you as humanity, and I want you as a person, to *keep* winning and play as big as you want. This book is about ways to do that.

THE JOY **and duty of doing what we love**

Doing what we love is a gift we give to each other, and give to ourselves.

Doing what really matters to us, as much as we can do it, is one of the best ways to be in contact with what is beautiful in life.

And also, doing what matters to us can bring up issues that we struggle with.

Altogether, that means doing what we want will bring us directly into contact with what's best for us to work on.

In a certain sense, I feel like as long as we're doing what matters most to us, it doesn't matter what that particular thing is. The *doing* of that, the pursuing of that path of joy, the exploration and improvement that brings, also improves *us*. It brings into sharp relief what we love and what we can work on in many other areas of our lives. Improving ourselves at one thing cannot help but improve us in some others. Achievement is not linear and is not confined to one track.

Do it for you. In every positive way, you deserve it. Don't hide your beauty from other people. Let yourself bloom. Enjoy it. Celebrate it. Love it.

Day Jobs Fund Art

Very few artists are born independently wealthy. And almost no artists are *immediately* financially self-supporting from their own art. In fact many of the works we consider high points of Western fine art were created during day jobs. Chaucer wrote *The Canterbury Tales* while working as a bureaucrat. Ernest Hemingway was a journalist. The abstract expressionist painter Jackson Pollock was a babysitter.

The brilliant minimalist composer Philip Glass worked as a taxi driver and a plumber, leading to this experience which can illustrate the day job experience quite well:

"I had gone to install a dishwasher in a loft in SoHo," he says. "While working, I suddenly heard a noise and looked up to find Robert Hughes, the art critic of Time magazine, staring at me in disbelief. 'But you're Philip Glass! What are you doing here?' It was obvious that I was installing his dishwasher and I told him I would soon be finished. 'But you are an artist,' he protested. I explained that I was an artist but that I was sometimes a plumber as well and that he should go away and let me finish."

https://www.theguardian.com/education/2001/nov/24/arts.
highereducation1

My day job is currently being a technical writer. This means I get to work out with words, sentences, clarity and understanding all day and then can do crazy things with those tools. So I also suggest looking at day jobs that might be close to what you love to create. You can be in it and breathe its atmosphere. Teaching is a fine vocation for a musician—also working as a guitar tech or drum tech, or recording engineer. Working in a gallery is a fine job for an artist—and also working in graphic design, or user experience. Or as an art critic for that matter.

Of course, these also aren't the only options. Bills must be paid, and being well compensated for the work you do serves a higher purpose. Many artists have had very straight jobs that were nowhere near their creative interests. Other artists have also found jobs that nudged them in the direction they wanted to go.

Whatever sort of day job you have, the more you can pursue your dreams and complete what you want then the happier and more beautiful the world can be.

Parenting and caregiving

To be very clear, parenting and caregiving are full-time jobs. They can and often involve working far more than 40-hours in a week; and even when there might be less hours, caretaking can often take up more than that share of a creator's mind simply because we love and care about people.

There can even be a share of guilt in doing something we want to and which we enjoy while someone we love and care for is hurting. It's completely understandable.

And also, in the best possible way, chuck that guilt to the side.

As the subtitle of this book states, we must balance what we want to do with what we need to do. When involved in the task of caregiving and supporting someone else, we must not abandon ourselves.

If it helps, consider that helping yourself be happy *is not only helping you, but* helping someone else. Your child benefits from knowing you care for them and help and love them, *and also* benefits from your example in your finding a way to do what you want. Any person you're taking care of benefits from you having the happiness and satisfaction you can have from creating in your own life. In general people who depend on you benefit from what they tell us all before taking off in airplanes–secure your own oxygen mask first.

And creating is often the oxygen for our spirits and souls.

DIFFERENT PHASES **of being a creator**

I'll mention this later, and also want to make this clear from the start: different methods will probably be useful at different phases of your creative experience. And even different times in your life, separate from your experience in creating.

Notice I didn't say levels or stages. This might be true for levels or stages too, and you will without question progress as you create more. You almost can't help it, progress is a natural result of doing something more like walking or talking. But progress is not always linear and not always immediately visible, and more to the point: what you need to create best can change regardless of your skill level. You might find yourself returning to methods you started a while ago that didn't work for you then, and might work for you now. You might find yourself trying something entirely new on a lark and get great results.

SIMPLE NOTIONS CAN BRING **up complex issues.**

I have come to a general conclusion in life: many things in life are simple. That by no means makes it easy. Sometimes the more effective a simple program is, the more it can bring up. It will surface things to work on. If what you want and what is happening are in sharp contrast to each other, then that provides a chance to learn something new and deep. What appears to be in the way can be the best kind of obstacle: a genuine opportunity to learn.

So if you are working on a task that matters to you and you're finding it difficult to take positive steps towards completing it, I invite you to consider where you are in the process *emotionally*. What might these difficulties suggest as an underlying cause? Are they bringing up doubts? Clashes? Motivations?

And then, don't overthink that. Think about it *just enough* to create a solution that will resolve this difficulty for *this specific task*.

Now if after that you come up with even more valuable insights and you're on a roll, by all means continue it. But if not, that's fine too.

To use an analogy, let's say you want to go for a hike and you find out your ankle hurts. You don't need to sign up for a personal trainer and work for a year to build up your legs to athletic perfection before you can go and enjoy that hike. All you might need is to find and buy a better set of hiking boots.

And you don't need to find the most perfect hiking boots in the world, and wander until you meet a Tibetan visionary who will help you form Timberlands from the hide of Pegasus. Changes are an off the rack pair from REI will do perfectly fine, and you can get straight to hiking right away.

Dropping things and catching them

All my life I've had a habit of becoming distracted to where I physically drop things. A few years ago, I noticed an interesting skill develop: I've gotten pretty good at catching them in mid-air.

Note that I am still dropping them. I haven't gotten better at that. Instead I've developed a secondary system to keep them from hitting the ground. This has been so useful it's been practiced over time, even without my realizing it. This compensating set of habits has been recorded to my synapses, and continues getting a bit quicker and smoother every time.

In the same way, the many different tasks involved in maintaining my day job, my creative work and my life can sometimes mean I momentarily forget something. I.e. I mentally drop it. In this area too,

I'm also continually improving at the skill of catching them before they hit the ground.

It could be nice in theory to stop dropping things entirely, and never forget anything. But having my mind so concretely focused on current details would also mean having less attention to spare for the things I want to imagine, to create, to do. The same habits that mean my focus can drift also result in many other things I quite enjoy. They leave me open to ideas that fascinate me, and new plans I can develop. This outlook even helps me in my day job, where I routinely make connections between information that other very smart people do not. And it leaves me open to benefit from the new ideas of others.

I might not be so creative and resourceful, and less able to enjoy the life I have and the world I'm blessed to be in, if I was too focused on never dropping things instead.

So I say, don't worry about when you drop things. And definitely don't beat yourself up about it, which benefits absolutely no one. Just catch things when you drop them, and continue to get better at catching them as you walk towards what you want in life.

To quote some of the wisest lines the Rolling Stones ever set to music:

> *You can't always get what you want,*
> > *But if you try sometimes*
> > *You just might find,*
> > *You get what you need*

It is always **about what works - and what *plays*.**

I heartily recommend trying things on and seeing what genuinely helps you do what you want to do. And just as heartily, if that something isn't helping, if it seems to slow or stop your creating or simply makes it too painful, consider trying something else. This is how I have assembled a patchwork quilt of methods, tools, and tactics that help me create.

Changing habits can be uncomfortable, and especially creative habits. I do want to emphasize that *no change you try has to be forever*. If you find you really aren't liking something, just go back to what you did before or take on something else. Now you know more about what works and plays for you. This is a great way to move forward as a creative and productive artist.

Ultimately, systems, methods and tools are useful only to the degree that they help you create. As I thought quite well stated by author Cassie Alexander, let's not fetishize the process. The process is not an end, but a means. The creative process is so we can create.

Let's create.

SECTION TAKEAWAYS

If I can sum this section up in one sentence: the best thing you can do for yourself, your art, your dreams and even the world is to care for and love yourself.

And not only in a passive way. Actively show yourself how seriously and lovingly your take yourself, by supporting yourself in doing the things you want. Like a good parent to yourself, be resourceful and clever and caring in how you find ways to give yourself the time and space to *be able to* create.

And then create.

With that, we're off!

CERTIFICATES

You'll find these at the end of every section in this book. Feel free to print them out if you like, and also to make your own. The certificates have a space for your name, but you don't need to fill it out. It's already certified true for you, by the simple action of checking out this book.

Certificate of Exploration

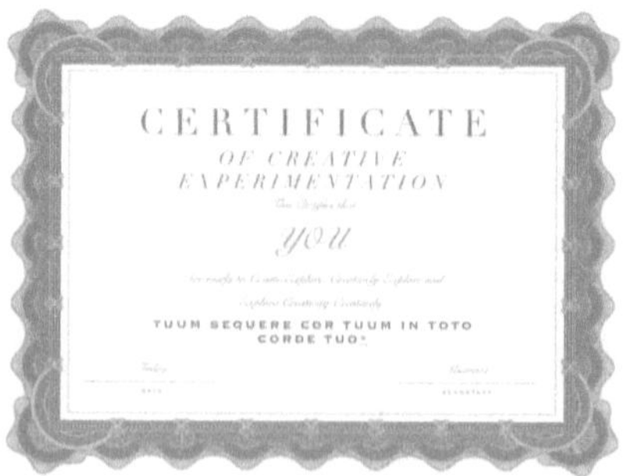

Permission Slip

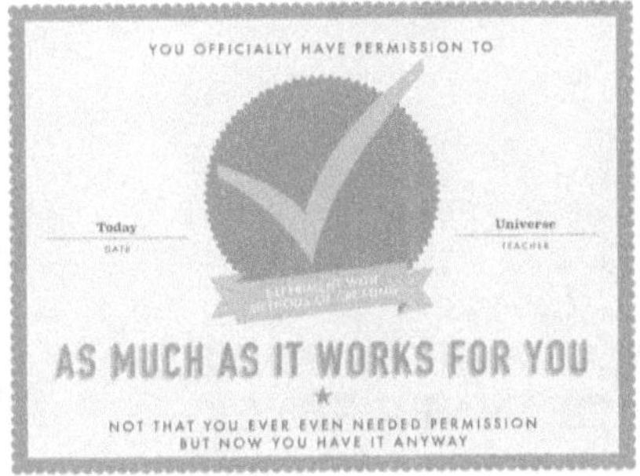
YOU OFFICIALLY HAVE PERMISSION TO
Today
DATE
Universe
TEACHER
AS MUCH AS IT WORKS FOR YOU
NOT THAT YOU EVER EVEN NEEDED PERMISSION
BUT NOW YOU HAVE IT ANYWAY

EMOTIONAL MANAGEMENT: THE NITTY GRITTY OF INNER SPACE

Creating a foundation for continued and sustainable productivity while doing work with most of your day.

This section is where we zoom in a bit and observe the forest where creation is taking place. The forest is beautiful, because it's you.

Creating consistently over time is beautiful, and like many beautiful things it can take work as well as play to make it happen.

Fortunately, like many other beautiful things, perfection is not required.

You can learn to be consistent and productive in your creative projects, while also being kind to yourself and doing the other needful things your life requires. In fact, this is what all artists learn. That's why it is different for each artist. The methods of productivity are as unique as you are.

And also, just like works of art can share letters, words, colors and notes used by other pieces and still be unique, so your methods of creative productivity can be made from the same tools other artists' use for their own creative production.

All that matters are that the methods help you create.

Some habits help provide foundations for other habits, as well as helping provide fuel for accomplishing tasks and helping us navigate our artistic and pragmatic lives. This section is about these meta-habits.

1. CLEARING THE DECKS

Motivation

Remember that you love this.

Find a way that you love it.

Remember that it can be hard effort. Remember and cherish when you get something done you wanted to do.

When creating music was on my front burner, getting a band to play for a roaring crowd was quite fulfilling. When I was pursuing photography foremost, completing pieces for a gallery show and then selling them put a smile on my face. Now that I'm writing, completing books and getting them in front of people who enjoy them can be the most satisfying part of every year.

That satisfaction is a grand reward all by itself.

Momentum = motivaction ™*

Also, a great way to be motivated is to keep momentum. Just do things. Just keeping that one sentence a day going when you don't feel like you can do a thing more can just help keep reminding you of this beautiful, glorious creative part of yourself. This is you, the real core essence of you.

I'm reminded of Alec Baldwin's epic "Coffee's for closers!" speech from the movie Glengarry Glen Ross. The man Baldwin portrays is a monster. But like a lot of frightening creatures, there's a fragment of wisdom that gives the character bite.

"ABC: Always Be Completing!" Always be taking some idea or project forward to complete it and share it with the world. And then on to the next one.

"Get mad, you sons of bitches!" If that's what it takes for you to do what you need to, then dig in to your defiance and do it!

Not a real trademark. At least not yet.

Cajoling

You can very often get yourself to do something if you just agree to do only a small bit of it. Like not washing all of the dishes, just one, and then you find yourself all the way over there by the sink so you might as well do a couple more, and then the whole thing is done.

There is many the time, bone tired, I got to the page just thinking I'd only write a single sentence or a couple of paragraphs, and managed to get out a thousand and even enjoy it.

Incrementalism

Every little bit helps. Do what you can when you can.

Consider setting intentions.

Setting intentions is a very simple thing that people have got a lot of utility from, as a way to clear the decks before creating.

An example of an intent can be, before you sit down to create:

"I will now write towards the end of this scene."

"I will paint a different kind of sky."

"I will try out some different chords to see what might work for a bridge."

"I will imagine playing keyboards as if I'm joking around with a sister."

"I will have fun exploring this character's reaction and response to a crazy situation."

Etc.

. . .

Fun with framing as fun

Consider what this is for. This is hard play. We all have had to work hard at some time in our lives, and likely still are now. Creating can be the fun opposite of that. We get to throw our effort into something that we enjoy.

You can do this at any level of intensity you want. I have found it worth doing this in pursuit of creative mastery. It's my opinion and experience that us humans getting good at something we enjoy is one of the best things in life. It almost doesn't matter what that thing is. As long as it's not actively harmful to others, it's good for us as a direct benefit that's quite distinct from the field we're gaining mastery in.

An expert archer, a passionate painter and an amateur musician are all engaged in the same rewarding endeavor: mastery as a pursuit.

I also like to consider the roots of the term "amateur –the <u>Latin word *amatorem*</u>, "one who loves". It literally means people doing what they love. Something which and thankfully very often does continue into professional levels of earning money. Put another way, there's no need for love of what we're doing to ever stop just because we're making money from it. And even if we're not making money from it, it's still very worth doing and needs no justification beyond the fact that we enjoy it.

(Now, very high levels of money can also mean fame which can become a difficult challenge of its own. I also consider that a good problem to have, and one that I'm very willing to take on the challenge of.)

What we tend to expect from professionals as opposed to amateurs, as we commonly use both terms, is a higher level of execution and detail.

It can also be fine if so. What we tend to forget is that the financially self-supporting artists we refer to as professional all started as amateurs.

Sometimes we hear from professionals who are unhappy, because in their pursuit of financial success they've lost the thread of what they loved. This is not some inevitable result, and it's not a reason to avoid professional success. One easy way to remove the potential complications of fame it simply to produce under an alias.

Fame and financial success can also be good problems to have. Like anything else in creative art or really any human endeavor, it can all mean a higher level of working on an understanding yourself. Which I like to consider a key reason for why we're here - and even if it's not then it's still a great thing to do until we find out better.

IF YOU STILL FEEL LIKE **you just can't that day**

Then don't.

You don't have to. None of this in this entire book fits in any way in a bucket labeled "have to".

Sometimes there is too much going on. Don't use your creative joy as another way to be mean to yourself.

I suggest you try it. And if you can't, come back to it the next day.

I was just this past weekend at a reading for a very successful fantasy writer. Let's call her Anne.

She related that in the past year she had deaths in her family and hip surgeries. She just didn't have it in her to write for a while. And so, with wisdom and compassion, she didn't further hold it against herself that she needed rest.

It's not a sprint, it's a walk.

It's not a perfect, it's a practice.

You might try just showing up and writing one simple thing. One page, one paragraph, one snippet of dialogue, one sentence.

You will work through what you need to. Until then, let yourself have the space you need.

What Anne found helped her was to show up to the empty page. If all she wrote was a single sentence, or even just a word, that was okay. Eventually she healed up what her creative heart needed to heal, and was able to write more and further while also keeping kindness and faith and love towards herself.

Whatever you do, do it with kindness and loving patience.

. . .

Pragmatic considerations

From a practical viewpoint, which again defined here includes kindness and compassion to yourself as the *literal* heart of practicality:

- how to keep workday emotions / emotional fallout from affecting or blocking creative time and production
- recovery time—figure out how much you tend to need, and give that to yourself in specifics. Maybe time out how much time it *can tend* to take, but don't hold yourself to it either way. When you're in that time, be 100% in that time. This is being with yourself with kindness and compassion time. Whether that's watching Netflix or staring at the wall.

One time I was so worn out I didn't even know what I needed, and I stopped by a diner and got a single cup of tea, and just stared at it for half an hour.

That was what I needed. No judgement, no complaints. Just sitting in being.

Understanding

Meditation

Meditation is the absolute easiest thing to do in life, on one level. It literally requires next to nothing.

The stats on the benefits of meditation are pretty clear. It is by no means some panacea that might cure all that ails someone. But it also has long term benefits in every area of life including longevity. Many different studies have shown its benefits to stress management, positivity, creativity, focus, memory and general health. In addition to helping in every other part of our life, help in those areas also aids the making of our art. Creative artists who have continually delivered excellence have made meditation a part of their regular habits, ranging from David Lynch to Jerry Seinfeld.

None of that makes it a panacea, of course. It does make it likely to be a very useful tool for most people, that's at least worth trying out.

I myself can have a hard time getting me to meditate. It can often show up as something "to do", when in fact it's the exact opposite of that. It might have something to do with a fear of being bored. I also have ADD, and meditation goes straight against that grain.

And like going to the gym, I *always* feel better after doing it and I have never once regretted having done it. It's just that, also like going to the gym, whenever I realize I have the free time so many other more important things tasks magically appear.

But still I find ways to do it, because it's just that great.

There are many different ways to meditate. The essential parts that I've found useful is:

- find a quiet spot where I can be left alone for 20 minutes or so
- sit down or lie down
- take a couple of deep breaths to let me know I'm in it
- find something to focus on that requires no conscious thought
- when thoughts inevitably arise, just let go of them and watch them go by like traffic, and return my focus to the thing that doesn't require any conscious thought

It's almost irritating how effective this can be at clearing out my own mental noise and stress. Perhaps I feel like I've really earned this mental noise, I can't let go of it that easy.

But I often can.

Three particular flavors of meditation that I've found useful are:

1. Transcendental meditation. Which is not something you have to spend a lot of money for. There's a cheap version of transcendental meditation that's worked quite well for me: https://www.n-srusa.org/home.php You can also find basic instructions on the Internet for free.

The essence is to find a syllable that doesn't have much other meaning as a word. Then repeat that word to yourself with no other intent but to relax.

2. Breathing. Similar to the above version of transcendental meditation, you simply become aware of breath and if any thoughts occur, you let go of them and sink into your own breath.

This method is great because breath is always there. It can connect you with your body in a way that your conscious mind needn't be engaged at all.

3. Feeling. This may be the simplest kind of meditation I've found. You just tune into how your body is feeling physically, starting in any place and going on until you've perceived all areas. From your toes all the way to the top of your scalp. Any thoughts that come up are noticed and let go of. This is great if you can be in your head like I can be.

There are many available books, apps and recordings for guided meditations. They range from entirely non-denominational to specific religions of your choice. As you'll read me saying multiple times throughout this book, it's all about what works - and what *plays*. What helps you to reconnect with the present and leave the work at work.

Sometimes it's **all about timing**

This method is almost like cheating. Work a job that takes a lot out of you so it's hard to do creative work in the evening? Do your creative play in the morning. :)

This can have a lot of benefits, not the least of which is setting yourself up for a good feeling the rest of the day. Of course, it can be tough to do all the time. The key, as always, is to treat yourself with kindness and compassion. Doing your creative work is something you're doing for you—it makes sense to carve out time where you can do it, just as it makes sense to carve out time to shower in the morning.

It doesn't only have to be in the morning. It can be lunch hour. It can be at your desk an hour early.

Or it can be notes accumulated during the whole day. People have written series of novels like this. With the advent of smartphones and software we can do this with an ease creatives of previous generations could only dream of.

And even in the pre-electronic times of the past, a notebook was always there. We humans are adaptable to many things. We can almost always find a way to make things work.

Consistency is important and helpful. Set it up. Look at your schedule and figure out that time, and then defend it. Let nothing else happen in that time. If you happen to get to that time and you don't feel like creating and nothing to tinker with, that's okay too. Just don't let other things take that time from you. Be there enough and the muse will find you and give you some things to work on.

And also, like any great lover, the muse doesn't need to be with you all the time. Your muse can appear and give you lovely fun and beautiful feelings and ideas, and leave you to savor them in the creation.

How to keep workday emotions / emotional fallout from getting in the work?

I suggest don't even try to keep the emotions out of it. Just create what you feel like creating. It will sort out in the next version of whatever you're making. Later on, as you look back on the art, you might not even know on which day you made what.

Other pursuits besides your main creative passion

Do other things you enjoy too. When you're not at work, you don't have to only pursue your front-burner passion. You can do other things that are just fun, because you enjoy them.

Not only do we need fun, and not only does having fun need no justification at all—but having fun is good for us. Fun is also good for what we want to create.

And also, we are entire universes and every part of what we learn to do can help every other part. I have a lot of fun in music and photography, and have for I think all of my life. Writing was always easiest and best for me as a full expression. But I learn other things about myself in other art forms—and I also learn things that apply to writing.

Working with music, for example, has let me marinate in that good feeling of really being in something that's very very satisfying—a feeling I now love and recognize when I'm writing something that's really lighting me up. Working with photography has introduced me to the great feeling of capturing a moment in the moment, and how people can look and shine in single moments.

I can at times struggle with having creative fun that isn't writing. I can spin my wheels making another electronica tune, or just whip up something strange in Photoshop just to get that idea out. I could also make myself feel guilty about that. I choose and strive not to.

In addition to the greatness of fun and enjoying life, this is a gift to the child and the artist in my soul. It's so important and good and just lovely fun to play. This is the fun challenge of adulthood—bringing grownup capabilities and strategies to the pursuit, attainment and maintenance of joy.

SIDE NOTE: BEING IN 'THE ZONE'

The zone, more formally described as the <u>flow state</u> or flow experience, is that state of being when someone is so deep in what they're doing that considerations of time and similar demands can fade. One becomes engrossed in the work, to the point that there seems less differentiation between the doer and the doing. This originally comes from studies of sports psychology, where it was noted that many athletes performed outstandingly well and even broke their own records in a state that wasn't quite intense conscious effort. If anything, it seemed that they had relaxed somewhat.

(A side note to the side note is that the athletes also often responded they felt that if they would try just a little bit harder they could have done better. Since this was actually the best that they had done, that seems unlikely. It seems more of their own guilt and expectations emerging that it "couldn't be this easy" – an interesting concept to look out for.)

This is a great and lovely state to be in, and the more often one gets to doing what one loves the more often one can experience that state. And also, getting into that state can be a fine sign that one is doing what one loves.

And also, quite a lot of our excellent writing is not in this state.

Sometimes we are just, as Stephen King put it, "shoveling shit from a sitting position."

The end result of what we're working on is largely made during this entire range of experiences – from ease and relaxation to teeth-gritting frustration, and points in between. The more often you write, the more often you will probably feel flow – and also I consider it worth writing if you don't.

However you choose to go about it, you can do it. Do it and get it done.

OTHER TOOLS

Journaling

I was first introduced to this method from the book The Artist's Way, which I heartily and thoroughly recommend. The method is simple: write in a notebook whatever pops into your head for three pages.

I found myself clearing through what was at the top levels in my mind and words, and going deeper into what I felt and what concerned me. I found this a great way to find out about myself, and a great low-intensity zero-risk way for me to try out anything I felt like. It didn't matter if it worked or not, or if anyone else ever saw it again.

You can of course do this electronically and not use a notebook. The benefits are in the connection to writing itself.

This is working out. Musicians and other performers practice, athletes stretch and lift weights. This is moving concepts and getting familiar with yourself as an artist. I thoroughly recommend this always.

And as always, don't feel bad if you don't do this. This is not an order and it is not a way to judge yourself. It's just something that's worked very well for me for a number of years.

VISUALIZATION

Visualization can be very useful for focusing and motivation. This visualization can be done in a range of methods, ranging from imagining with eyes closed to outward manifestations like dream and vision boards.

Whatever method of visualization we engage in, it can be very useful to consider what you are visualizing. Results seem to be much better when people aren't solely visualizing outcomes, and instead are visualizing *taking steps to achieve* those outcomes.

A great thing about scientific study is when it surfaces a twist that can be somewhat counter-intuitive. In this case, studies appear to indicate that visualization works best when you imagine steps you need to take. In a real-world example, envisioning passing a test can *lower* your score, as that might make you feel you don't need to study. Envisioning *studying* for that test can put the need for that step in your mind, resulting in more study and a better grade.

With that caveat in mind, and a note that your own creative mileage may vary, a dream or vision board can also be a good way to carve out space for your creativity, and declare it. Even if you are declaring it to yourself.

The flip side is not to take the visualization as a substitute for taking on and completing specific things. Sometimes our brains can take thinking about doing something as close enough to do it. This can actually work well for rehearsing physical tasks such as acrobatic moves or dance. But it's never a substitute for performing the actual moves.

That said, inspire yourself! Whatever helps get you to the most productive mood.

PODCASTS and YouTube casts

Podcasts can be powerful, inspiring and very motivating. I generally don't listen to them during my day job, as my day job also involves a lot of writing. I did find a way to listen to podcasts during my driving commute. It was a great way to keep my motivation up and keep me focused while I was performing my day job.

Regular podcast has many benefits beyond the direct transfer of information. Listening to people speak on a topic that I'm deeply interested in helps to inspire me. When one of the first things I hear in the day is inspires me, and it helps frame my whole day.

Besides Apple's iTunes, Spotify and similar services to download and listen to podcasts, I'm a big fan of standalone apps such as Dogg-Catcher and Stitcher. There's also plenty of excellent motivational and instructional videos on YouTube, a truly deep resource that provides great rewards from time spent sorting through the chaff.

You can find a short list of specific recommendations for podcasts in the "Further Resources" section towards the back of this book.

A FINAL NOTE **on encouragement**

I think that waiting until you really feel like it to start doing what you want, is often waiting longer than you need to.

Really feeling like doing something that matters to you is great, and that feeling really isn't a requirement. Also, a great amount of that feeling can often come once you get over the initial resistance to starting the task, and you're actively engaged in doing.

Ultimately, you deserve to believe in yourself. And also, the world is really great and wonderful enough that *you don't need to believe in yourself in order to succeed.*

It's great when you believe in yourself. It makes everything easier and better.

But all you really need to do is do things.

So encourage yourself. And also, I heartily recommend that if you don't necessarily feel encouraged, or if you don't know if you're encouraged enough--*go ahead anyway.*

And get on to building those habits and doing things.

2. BUILDING HABITS AND REMOVING BLOCKS

For a good view on building habits, I'm indebted to the writer James Clear. These principles apply to any art, whether writing, painting, songs or sculpture.

The essentials are:

1. Start with an incredibly small habit.

Pick a small action, and set up to perform it consistently and persistently. Write a single paragraph. Make a single pencil sketch. Create a single musical riff or series of chords.

2. Increase this habit in small ways

Writing a paragraph a day for a week? Great. Go for two paragraphs a day. The average number of words on a printed paperback page is about 350, and the average number of words in a paragraph is 150. Averaging two paragraphs a day can mean writing a printed page a day--which is fantastic. At that rate you're already at one full first draft of a mid-sized novel a year.

The same for visual art and music. Create two sketches a day, or add a one new color to an existing sketch a day. Create two riffs or short pieces of music, and then jam them together. How do they work? Is it fun?

3. As you build up habits, break them into smaller chunks

For a writing example, want to get to writing a full page a day? You can try writing one paragraph every four hours. This quickly has you at a speed of one first draft of a *big* novel a year--600 pages.

For visual art and music, this is well over 300 pieces a year. You may not even like most of them. But if you're creating at that amount, you can't help but have more than a few that you will really love. This can point the way forward, not only in your skill and execution but in trying on things you might have taken much longer to have a chance to try.

4. When you slip, dust yourself off and get right back on the horse

Of course, and as I'll say in a myriad of ways throughout this book, at some points you'll slip off your ideal schedule, miss steps in your plan, and so forth. That's fine. The schedule is not a stick to beat yourself into obedience with. It's a way to help you find a track you can work with, and see when you're not on it so you can get back on it and do more of what you want to do.

Remember the ultimate goal is doing and making what you want. This is a kindness to you, as you deserve to do what you want. And it is a kindness to the world, in helping you follow your inspiration to create and refine your gift to the world. None of that is about being mean to yourself.

Detecting and healing blocks

Blocks can be tricky. Sometimes there are just very legitimate reasons why we aren't getting to a thing we want to do. Some days all 24 hours are taken up doing genuinely needful things. Self-care is always important, and that includes downtime.

And other times, what is behind our not doing the things we want to do is fear. The reasons which we are coming up that we can't do what we want "right now" are more akin to rationalizations for avoiding what we want.

From my experience blocks definitely become clear over time.

Like scientists detecting black holes in space by seeing their effect on the visible stars around them, you can see your own blocks by looking at what isn't getting done over what is.

For example, if you find yourself watching TV for hours after work for weeks at a time but aren't setting the time to follow up on creating your art for twenty minutes, you are most likely dealing with a block. Similarly for ending the first draft of that story—times like those are when blocks can really start showing up.

One these blocks are identified, it can be easy to be very frustrated with them. It's important to consider that these blocks are the visible parts of defense mechanisms. As frustrating as they can be, they are parts of you which are actively trying to protect you. They come from very young parts of yourself, and worked to give you the protection that young you thought you needed at the time. They just aren't calibrated properly for what you want to do.

When these parts of yourself become visible, see them with compassion. And at the same time work and play through them. Behind them is usually something that just needs to be heard and reassured.

And also, don't use these blocks as a reason not to create at all. That probably is another way a block is being tricksy.

HEALING POTENTIAL BLOCKS **in your flow**

There are many possible and non-exclusive approaches to clearing blocks. They generally sort into five categories:

1. work directly on what might be stopping you
2. work in spite of what might be stopping you
3. work with what's stopping you so it works for you
4. work on something else than the current project you're stopped on until that other project is complete, then come back
5. work on something else until/unless you're stopped on

that other project, and switch back and forth until one or both projects are done.

...You can work with all of those. Or you can work with something else.

I feel like I can heartily recommend 2) – it will lead you into 1) as needed, and might bring you to an understanding that can enable some 3) as well. This is one path you can waltz through creation to a fuller understanding of yourself.

What I can always recommend is making sure that you're always in forward creative motion. Only you can determine what that is for you.

Kindness and compassion

Art is hard work as well as play. It's real effort and it takes us to the most human part of ourselves, even when it's simple fun...even *because* it can be simple fun.

I hold to the notion of kindness and compassion to ourselves as we do this thing. We don't need to deserve our love in order to "earn" our own love. And we deserve it anyway. Let us not be harsh taskmasters with ourselves. Let us be midwives to ourselves and what we're giving birth to. Metaphorically, analogously, that's what's happening here. Let us be kind and practical and supporting and encouraging and ask of ourselves a deeper level of mastery through production. And let us love ourselves and not be mad when we don't hit our goals, and we only gain the mountaintops instead of the stars. Next time, we can aim for the stars again.

Consider the work of making the work...it isn't really work. It's effort, in pursuit of fun or insight or humor or a change of pace, or other things, or all of the above.

Consider the play.

· · ·

FEELINGS

What we create as art cannot help but be affected by our feelings. Everything in life, really. But specifically, what we create.

So probably the best thing you can do for your art, as well as most certainly your life, is to feel your emotions, accept them and get familiar with them. Something that can be difficult for many of us in working situations where we are encouraged to push our feelings to the side.

Now there are very pragmatic reasons for why we often do this with our feelings. It will probably cause difficulties if we tell off that entitled customer, or if they even know we're mad. If someone is a nurse, someone who is difficult still needs care. If someone is working in a factory, their boss being a jerk isn't enough pragmatic reason to follow one's feelings and punch them out or quit.

The price that can be paid for this necessity is that when we are done with our day or have a period in which we can do something we truly want to do, these feelings can return. Having been stuffed down all day from need, they can come back up once we're in a space where we can want. What to do with them?

Often the best thing we can do is: take a break and actually feel them. We've been ignoring them, and now they want our attention – and our feelings aren't coming from elsewhere. 'They' are us.

And feeling them means not judging them, which can get complicated very quickly. It can mean not judging the part of us that wants to judge them. But the way it's complicated can be similarly to unclenching a muscle one didn't realize one was holding tight all day. It's a skill that can be developed, and a habit that I think is very worth developing.

Feeling your feelings is not indulging them, in a negative sense. It's acknowledging them. It's acknowledging and honoring you, and your own humanity.

So much of beauty and art and creativity is feeling. Feeling is such an integral part of the gift you're giving yourself, and others, when you're in your creativity. Which is not to make it too lofty either. Just lofty enough! It's also just fun. It's also just a damn blast to make something fun that has you in it, that comes from you, that is feeling real and your real feelings are in. It connects us to ourselves, and connects ourselves to others, across space and time. When we look at the magnificent cave paintings of Lascaux we know we are seeing a human being much like us, across the chasm of ten thousand years.

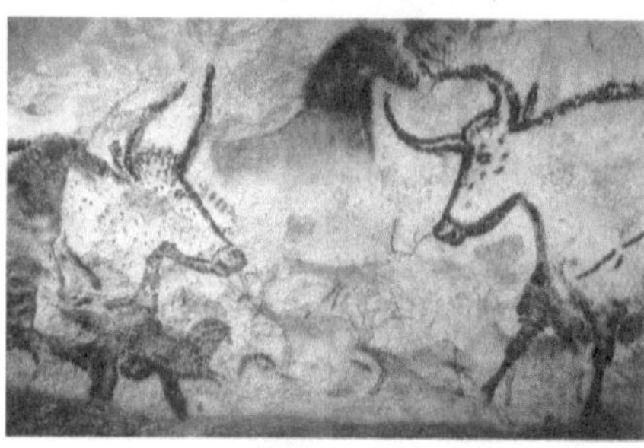

Go ahead and feel the parts of yourself that want to feel, and treat the parts of yourself that are feeling those ways with love, kindness and compassion.

Kindness and compassion for yourself in other ways

Which is another note: improving any one thing in your life almost can't help but improve all of it. No one of us is ever involved in only one thing at a time. We are wholes; we are systems.

Getting the sleep you need improves everything. Getting the nutrition you need, the exercise and the air that makes your body feel good. Cleaning the bathroom. Making any part of your life better improves everything else in it.

And the one thing that really improves everything, and it's so simple and it can be so hard to do:

Love yourself. Have kindness and compassion for yourself.

And those parts of you that are really mad and are maybe yelling at you to do more? This can be difficult to navigate but I have found it very healthy and good for me:

Have kindness and compassion for those parts too.

Those are defense mechanisms. They likely developed at a very young part in your life when it was how you knew to protect yourself. Those are parts of you that are trying to protect you.

You don't have to do what they say. You can listen to them and hear them. They are parts of you, the child you, and you can feel them and hear them without having to act on them.

In fact, pragmatically speaking, being with them with love and compassion and thanking them for sharing is a great way to help keep them from interrupting you when you're doing what you want.

But more than just the pragmatism, those defense mechanisms are you and deserve love and compassion. You just don't have to do what they say. And a lot of us are taught by example that the best way to deal with them is just to not listen at all. To stuff those feelings and the parts of us they come from down in a hole.

Which doesn't work. That just makes them more likely to explode. Bring them listening, love and healing instead.

Annoyingly enough, many times the hippies are exactly right. This is one of those times: love, kindness and compassion are what we need. Bring love and kindness and compassion to the child inside you that wants to make and create and share beautiful things with the world. Or any similar way you feel about creating, in your words or feelings.

It's all about what works, with "bringing kindness and compassion to yourself" key to determining how well it works.

BOTTOM LINE: **in practice**

In practice, I have found that feeling things takes away their power over me. Like a lot of writers and artists in general, one way I dealt with emotions that weren't convenient to feel was to intellectualize them - to make abstractions of them so I could sort through them. This has the survival benefit of offering a strategic way of dealing with difficult situations with some added clarity. It has the downside of distancing you from your own emotions, feelings, and even sensations.

It can be tough to face these feelings. As described to me, it can feel similar to the sensation of bringing blood back to your hands after they've been frozen or fallen asleep. The return can be accompanied by discomfort.

Kindness and compassion for yourself and all of you that is feeling is the best way forward that I know. It not only frees you for your art, it acquaints you with yourself. And you yourself are beautiful, and worth seeing yourself as a gift to you.

3. WORKING WITH EMOTIONS

The stages of creation

The act of creation can make us feel vulnerable and activated, and the resulting emotions can manifest in many ways in our lives. These emotions can also be managed in many ways.

Legendary science fiction author Robert Heinlein once closed an article on writing with five rules for a successful professional writing career. The rest of the article before them is excellent, but it has not had the impact that these five rules have had.

As with other examples, the details are given in terms of writing, but the principles fit pretty well with most any form of artistic creation.

1. You Must Write.
2. Finish What You Start.
3. You Must Refrain From Rewriting, Except to Editorial Order.
4. You Must Put Your Story on the Market.
5. You Must Keep it on the Market until it has Sold.

On looking at this recently I was reminded of the 5 stages of grief as noted by the psychiatrists Kübler-Ross. For the unfamiliar, these are the typical stages most humans can go through when they are grieving something particularly difficult:

Denial > Anger > Bargaining > Depression > Acceptance

Just for the heck of it I thought I might put them together in a table and see how they relate. It turns out they map to my own emotional experiences almost perfectly.

Heinlein's 5 rules of writing + Kübler-Ross 5 stages of grief

= How we can sometimes feel about the stage of the story we're writing

Heinlein's 5 rules of writing	+ Kübler-Ross 5 stages of grief	= Common stages of emotions during a creative project
You Must Write	Denial	It's impossible to find time to create!
Finish What You Start	Anger	I won't finish it and you can't make me!
You Must Refrain From Rewriting, Except to Editorial Order	Bargaining	Can't I keep revising it?
You Must Put Your Story on the Market	Depression	I don't want to put it out.
You Must Keep it on the Market until it has Sold.	Acceptance	I've released it to the world, and I'm ready to move on to the next story.

THE LESSON FOR ME, the lesson is twofold:

1. How I feel at any moment during a project can just be a natural consequence of the stage I'm in, and doesn't necessarily have anything to do with negatives of the project.
2. It's perfectly appropriate and even *good* to feel these ways, as part of moving on to the next phase of the project.

By understanding what stage of creation I'm in, I'm better able to understand and connect with what I'm experiencing. The idea is not to suppress those emotions, which we can so easily do. Nor is it to pile criticism on top of those emotions. Instead a process of under-standing the emotions and how they relate to our process can help us have compassion for ourselves. By understanding what we're experiencing, we can better treat ourselves with kindness and give our feelings the understanding and attention they deserve.

Besides being good to ourselves, which is all the justification needed just by itself, this way of being has a pragmatic benefit. It keeps our inner rebel from derailing what we, including the rebel, wants to do.

I sometimes think of my feelings as my fellow passenger in our road trip. If I pay attention to my feelings and just acknowledge them, they are less likely to fight for the wheel. And I am also more likely to hear interesting ideas and suggestions, and get to somewhere we both want to go.

Stress from your non-creative life

Stress in other parts of your life is tough. Creating is fun and life-affirming, almost no matter how dark the subject might be. (I'm tempted to say 'no matter how dark', but I am trying to shy away from absolute statements. This is at least partly because I expect many writers will treat absolute statements like I do - immediately start exploring edge cases to disprove them.)

Find a way to have fun. Just do that. Boss is being a jerk? Imagine a world where you have power over them. Or a world where they're not allowed. Or a world that is so far removed from them that they might as well not exist. Find a fun place to play and play.

And also, if you don't feel like creating, you don't have to. I do suggest this: find at least some little thing to do, even if it's just write a new sentence or fix some punctuation, and do that. Just that little bit, every day. Not in a way that tries to stifle or deny they real things you're doing. Just in a way that also honors that part of you that wants to create, and gives that part of you a nice fun thing too.

DEALING WITH BLAME, **shame and other feelings that just aren't fun**

Feel them, practice not judging them. You don't have to go with them or against them. I've found Buddhism in general to be a fantastically effective way of working with myself compassionately so I can be with myself and feel these feelings, and not going to either negative pole of a) shutting them down and cutting myself off from life or b) completely turning myself over to impulse regardless of consequences and becoming an asshole.

DEALING with anger

Anger is not fun to feel. But it's real and we have it for a reason. Among other things it brings positive power to it: a motivation to create and keep needed healthy boundaries, and a fuel for defiance.

The original title of this entire book was: "...And the Horseshit You Rode In on." Subtitle: "How to go ahead and create things, when hours after work you're still so mad you're punching things."

That should show you how I felt about my job at the time. If you don't like your day job, let me tell you, I have *been* there.

You can be mad without others being wrong *or* you being wrong. More to the point being mad is a feeling to be felt. It can be worth understanding what you are reacting to. But the feeling itself doesn't need to be justified and doesn't need to be acted on – just acknowledged. It is coming from a part of you, one that is trying to protect you. Let yourself feel it, and treat that part of yourself with loving kindness and compassion. It is worth it because it is you, and you are worth it.

PROCRASTINATION...

A big ugly word for a small thing. Like anything that's neglected procrastination can grow, but at its heart it's quite simple. Procrastination usually comes from a shyness about doing the things you want to do. This in turn often comes not from a fear of failure--but fear of success.

What if you did those things that you wanted to do? How might doing those things change the way you have thought life should be defined, bordered, safely contained? How might that alter the beliefs or habits that others told you, or that you have accumulated in much younger attempts to make sense of the world?

Let's hold compassion for this part of us that is afraid, and cajole ourselves forward to find out what we can do.

....AND PROCRASTINACTION!

Besides the method of working with what I'm feeling directly, I have had some fun employing a method I like to call procrastin*action*. Don't want to do a thing right now that you also want to really do? That's fine. Get something else done. Clean the dishes. Organize the garage. Do some push-ups. Email an old friend.

That's a side bucket of action, not a strategy. But it can be fine too.

And then, get back to creating.

WORKING with our demons

In a similar way we can work with your demons. The pros and cons of this in practice can look like this:

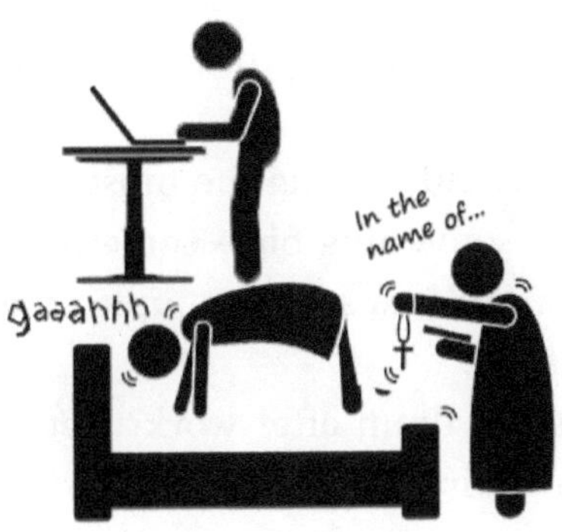

NOTICE the writer on top is getting some good work done with their demon – but the platform is not stable. The demon is unpredictable. And if the demon is actually healed, or even becomes less of a problem, the guy can drop and even fall.

Also the writer doesn't have the best posture.

Long term healing and reconciling with our demons is the best way to go. And also, doing what you want to and creating what you want can be a great way to help that healing as well.

You're not only creating in order to help yourself heal, OR only healing just to help yourself create. You are one entire universe. Every good thing you do and even good way of being towards you helps every other thing in you. And not that it even needs this justification, but also that helps every person outside you.

Conserving will?

There are some interesting theories and studies that model willpower as an expendable resource that's even a physical one, or at least neurological. I think there is some utility in this. It can be worth considering when your willpower might be low, and it can be very worth setting up plans and processes that leave you more of it. This can (and is great if it does) include areas of your life that have no seeming direct relation to creativity. This is an example of something improving in a seemingly entirely different area of your life then improving creativity too.

Look at what is currently taking the most willpower in your life. Or the most time. Not something big – something *small* that's occurring as an annoyance. And just see if a couple of quick steps will take this stone from your shoe.

Doing the dishes is a drain after work? Get paper plates. Doing your own taxes is a drain? Pay someone to do them. (I've almost always saved more money than this cost too.)

You're saving up will. You're going to have more of it, and it's going to be good for you even besides what you create.

A checklist of compassion methods

We can actually work at showing more kindness and compassion to ourselves. These have actually worked for me, as ways to expand both my current amount of good feeling and my capacity to receive and store it.

- **Literally pat yourself on the back.**

Why shouldn't you have your own approval and support? When I get something done that I've wanted to for a while, or was tough, or was new or quite fun, I extend my hand past my shoulder and pat my own back. It can be a good, mellow feeling that I can always afford to give myself.

- **Take compliments from others.**

We can be in a habit of being polite and returning compliments right back to people who give them, as if it was a tennis match. Of course, genuine compliments are worthy of appreciation in their own right. But also, it is a genuine gift to others to let yourself receive the compliment and accept it. It is allowing others to contribute to you, which they want to do because they genuinely appreciate you.

So as hard as it can be to get used to, I suggest you grit your teeth and accept the compliment without immediately returning it. Stand and take it like the worthy person you are.

The risk: you might start emotionally realizing your own excellence.

- **Share what you're doing with people who appreciate it.**

People who suck and suck your energy don't deserve to know and don't need to know squat.

People who are great and supportive and just in general helpful and not critical – let them know what you're doing so they can get a chance to appreciate it. People who care for you will dig it and appreciate how you are letting your light shine. Besides sharing the light of you, it gives them inspiration for doing what they want to do as well.

- **A mantra**

When I've felt troubled and about to get into it with my defense mechanisms instead of letting them play in a vast field that I'm not attached to, I've repeated this mantra. It's a two-parter:

1. Kindness and compassion to myself.
2. Kindness and compassion to others *as long as* it doesn't violate kindness to myself.

If that phrase seems like it might be useful to you, maybe try it on. If not that, then maybe try something else. Some sort of a reminder of being kind to ourselves can be a good and useful thing. It is bringing the power of kindness to ourselves, from ourselves, in the real moment that we are in.

A Game of Don'ts

Here are some things I consider great to not do.

1. Don't ever use money as a yardstick for how good you are.

I cover money from creativity more extensively in a later section, but it's important enough that I wanted to mention it here first.

US culture in particular can use money as a blunt metric for intrinsic value, with often absurd results.

Now, money and value also don't have to be at odds. 'Selling out' as it's often cynically called is not necessarily the only way to sell. The money can be a means to that end – and it also can be another fun way to play the game. But it is most definitely not the end.

Following that through, just as money is not itself a measurement of success, *lack* of money is not a measurement of *failure.*

Every bit that you get to enjoy something is a lovely victory worth relishing and thanking yourself and the universe that made it possible.

And if you want, you can look to find ways to make money from it as another part of the game.

2. Don't negatively compare yourself to your idols or their peers.

Learn from their process, pick up things you want to try, gain inspiration from their work-- but through it all, remember you are your own artistic universe.

3. Remember your heroes final works were not their first versions.

The works of art you read, experience and loved are the polished results of massive amounts of unseen effort. Very often this effort has involved more people than the titled author—several different kinds of editors, proofreaders, book designers, and more. As only one example, the legendary novel we know as "To Kill a Mockingbird" was Harper Lee's *second* version of that novel. This book that has achieved world fame for decades was based from chunks pulled from her first draft, and then overhauled extensively from a publishing house editor's notes into the entirely different work we know today.

Writing is far from the only art form where this occurs. In painting, the old masters revised layers and layers of paintings as they created what we rightly now consider masterpieces. Throughout his career, Picasso would continue to push his paintings with further revisions and alterations, to sometimes find out he'd pushed it too far and just let it go. (For a unique look at Picasso's creative process in live action, see "The Mystery of Picasso" in the "Web Links" section of this book).

There are very rare cases in music where lightning was captured in a bottle. Even in those cases, such as recorded live performances by masters such as Jimi Hendrix, Miles Davis or John Coltrane, getting to that point where they could channel a complete work in real time came after years of dedicated effort and passionate pursuit. What you are not hearing there is the many different takes before then, all the efforts and failures over years, all to develop the skill for the tools to keep up with the mind and to fix notes going wrong in real time. We are only experiencing the final product.

SECTION TAKEAWAYS

Creating the foundation to help make what we want can be a creative process all to itself. And as such it can, will and should look slightly different for every person.

We've gone over the many different tools, which can be used in any order and to any degree that works for you. These tools include:

- Reframing
- Meditation
- Building specific task-based habits
- Detecting and healing blocks
- Working with specific emotions

What remains most important, as always, is what works for you.

Ready to go further?

Great! Looking forward to meeting up at the start of the next chapter.

CERTIFICATES

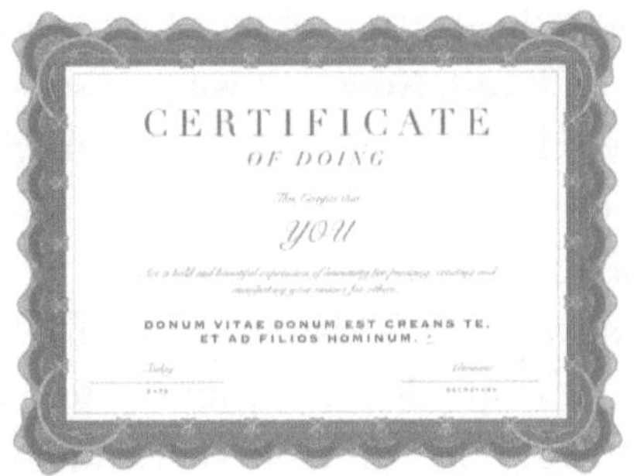

Permission Slip

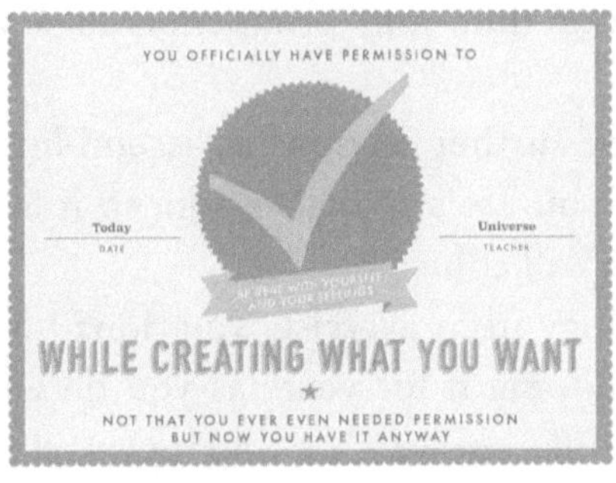

CREATION MANAGEMENT: LIVING IN SPACE AND TIME AROUND YOU

In this part, we come down from higher levels of abstraction to just above the trees in the forest. Now that we've discussed meta concerns and meta habits, let's look at some strategies and processes that can help your regular creative production and measurable productivity, while doing day job work for most of your day.

It's great to be alive, and it's also often vexing. These two poles of our experience of life come directly from the foundations that make life both possible and at times difficult: space and time.

It behooves us to find ways to optimize our time on this earth towards what inspires us, and to be as productive in that realm as we can within that time. With creative work in particular, this can also mean managing our time and production in a way that nurtures our joy.

Look at this and further sections as assembling the quilt of what works for you. As you are a living person, so it is a living quilt. You will change, so you will adjust it.

To use an analogy from exercise, you don't lift the same weights when you've been doing it for years as you do when you just start. You will be lifting different weights, and may well have changed your exercises also.

4. PROCESSES

Keep It Simple, Superhero

Many things in life are simple. That doesn't make them easy – but it can at least make them clear.

If you don't yet have a process, then feel free to skip this section and write. After you've created a few things you'll most likely have noticed some ways that you tend to work.

And when you find a process is working, it's fine to stay with it. Don't feel a need to interrupt or change a plan that's producing well for you.

If you do find yourself feeling restless with a current process or playflow (not quite the same as a workflow), it will probably be useful to look at your process.

Top consideration: **time and knowing thyself**

It's great to push one's own limits to find what they are, as that also gives the chance to expand them.

And also, I implore you to keep this in the context of kindness and compassion for one's self.

Using myself as an example, even when I have a whole day free such as a weekend, it can be really hard for me to keep writing straight for more than 5 hours. So, it would in theory be great if I could make up a week's worth of words on both days during the weekend. In practice, this isn't where I'm at.

So I can work on expanding how many hours straight I can write (and I am).

But also, the more I can free up other time to write the better. Among other things, I don't want to only be dependent on having that time free. It's not predictably reliable that I'll be free every weekend.

That's also why I so highly recommend exploring creation in increments, steps and moments. It all adds together.

Approaching your takeoff

Below are some high-level ways to see your creative approach. Try on any that seem useful. Some of them may, and some of them definitely are, "Captain Obvious" level items. They're also proven methods that creatives all over the world have put into their toolkit to get what they want done. I expect that at least some of them will work for you, and work more for you the more that you do them.

There are few things as simple as doing push ups or walking to stay in shape. They work too.

What is your process?

What are the steps you took and the phases you went through to reach the end of that first draft?

Once you've written down all the steps, and if you're like me adding in some that you hadn't initially realized were there - add in the time involved to do each task right.

Now look at what takes the most time. How might that be streamlined? Would parting that out help? Or maybe you have some revisions that occur before you make some other changes – thus requiring more revisions. Perhaps the process can be reordered so there's only one set of revisions instead of two?

No need to overthink it. Think it just enough. This isn't to overwhelm you, it's to keep you from feeling overwhelmed and to set you up for success.

For example, when most recently looking at my own process in fiction work I found that worldbuilding is causing a lot of rewriting for me. I can fall in love with an idea and jump all the way in with both feet–then to find out halfway in that the world needs to work at a higher level of detail than I thought. I have to pause my forward writing motion to resolve contradictions, and then rewrite scenes that were otherwise functioning just fine.

Some part of this is tough to avoid. We don't always know the path until we start the journey.

On the other hand, the more of the worldbuilding I resolve earlier then the less time I can spend on structural reworking and the more I can concentrate on story.

WAYS TO EXPLORE **your process**

- Write down your process on paper, as a series of steps. Even if you already are sure you know it, there is a clarity that can emerge from seeing it in words.
- Now that you can see it, see how you can simplify it. Make the process as simple as you can (but not simpler). Is there a step you can pull out, or a couple of steps you can combine? Is there another approach to the same set of steps that might simplify things?
- Next try to make things as easy as you can (but not easier). See if there's a way to do one step or part of your process with less effort. Would a different order help? Could a couple of steps actually be done in parallel?

Almost all creative processes, and I'm tempted to say all, consist of repeating sets of individual actions. These actions are just applied with increasing insight and skill as we get used to performing them.

This also means that removing even a single unnecessary action from a regular process can be a very significant savings in time, effort and resource over the course of a week, a month or a year.

How do your heroes do it?

It's always interesting to find those people whose work you love, and research how they make that work.

Key caveat: *only look at your heroes in helpful ways.* Don't psych yourself out. Just take some of your favorite artists in the field you want to create in, and read up on what their actual working processes are. They will almost certainly end up creating differently than you in some ways–and there are some parts of their process which will be useful for you to check out. You know they've worked well for somebody, so odds are they're at least worth looking at.

In saying that, none of that means their processes can work entirely for others. Their processes might not work at all for others. Some artists are just legitimate freaks of nature in every good way, such as the incredible Jack Vance. Others have genius-level writing combined with personal demons that worked them to the bone to produce, like Philip K. Dick. That doesn't have to be you. I'm very much opposed to the myth of the "tortured artist" as the only way for great art to occur. Many artists have been quite productive all their lives, with no more ups and downs than anyone else. J.R.R. Tolkien comes to mind, as does Robert Heinlein and TV legend Stephen J. Cannell.

Keep in mind that your heroes had day jobs

As we do look at our heroes, it's useful again to remember that they walked the earth as we did while they developed their art and put their production processes together. I started off this book with a few examples. Here are a couple more. Stephen King had a day job for years as a school teacher. Jimi Hendrix was a back-up guitarist for Little Richard, making peanuts as a touring musician for years. All the Bronte Sisters, working as governesses.

Take the good from that. If you don't have to work a day job, then don't. :) There is no shame in your success or good fortune in other realms. Just understand that if you do have a day job now, you are in good company. And not only good – you are in the company of some of the greatest artists humanity has produced.

WORKING with yourself and what might be in your way

Within all of this, it might be useful to consider working with your creative self as you would with a truly beloved employee. The processes you're looking at aren't a way to try and squeeze the last drop of profit out. You're looking for a way to make your creative work easier, a way to amplify your efforts.

So be the best possible boss for yourself, and see how you can best set yourself up for your own success.

A particular way that this approach worked well for me was with the idea of Attention Deficit Disorder. For years I was very skeptical about ADD even being a real thing. It just seemed too convenient a way to explain a lot of ways that completing tasks can be difficult for anyone. I even wondered if it was an example of a medical tendency towards pharmaceutical prescriptions as solutions. All through the same period I was also very hard on myself for not completing more than I was.

Then as a lark I took a simple online test for ADD, where answering 'yes' to 12 out of 25 questions meant I likely had it. I answered 'yes' to 13. So from that point I tried an experiment. Just to see how it would go, I treated myself *as if* I had ADD.

I set up systems to help myself, and consulted doctors and counselors that I could afford at the time. I was even prescribed Adderall for a bit.

Since this experiment my life has been simpler, easier, less unpleasant and more productive. Not just my creative life, but my entire life. I ended up not taking Adderall regularly, but I did gain from that experience what a fuller focus can be like. Now I know when I'm *not* concentrating as much as I can, and I can address that or work around it.

Now, does that mean I actually have ADD? If I do, I have a light touch of it. From a very practical standpoint, it *doesn't matter* if I have ADD or not. What matters is that in trying a set of things, I found some ways that worked well and have really helped me out.

As a variant of this, sometimes when I'm looking at a process I like to imagine, in the best possible way of course: how would I do this if I were smarter? And then see what I come up with.

Try it on for size

Try it on and see for a specific period of time you set beforehand. If you find you don't like it or it doesn't seem to produce results you like, then feel free to ditch it and try something else.

If it does seem to work and it doesn't seem destructive, try more of it. If it doesn't work, don't feel that you have to do it at all ever again.

You can just cross it out. :)

Also keep aware that different things can work at different times both in your life. It might be just right for the place you are right now, or it might have been for a particular stage in your creative path but not necessarily others. Or some combination of all of the above, or something else.

There is almost certainly no single answer that will always be right.

The flip side of this is that there are any number of different ways that will work at least some little bit better.

Keep blame entirely out of it

It is all about what works – or perhaps even more accurately, what *plays.* Play isn't necessarily easy all the time, either. Skill at any endeavor takes effort, difficulty, discomfort. It's also fun overall even if it may not be fun right now. Like all the effort expended learning to walk, or to speak, or to draw, or to kiss.

5. TIME AND PLANNING

Know thy schedule, know thyself. Learn thy process, learn what can work for thyself.

WHAT ARE your best times to create?

Is your schedule solid, or constantly shifting? If you're a parent or caregiver, it may be more shifting than solid.

Whatever you have, work with it. Right as you start creating, note the time and the place. Do this for a couple of weeks. If you can, when the time is up or you have to do something else jot down how many words or pages you happened to get done.

Once you've accumulated some information, say two weeks or 10 sessions, you have some data to review. Look back over it. Were there common trends? What circumstances felt easiest, and also what circumstances seemed the most productive?

This information can help you in the next step: planning out your plan.

PLAN TO FIND your plan

This consideration can be trippy. What's the best way to plan the best way to plan? Would that mean you should plan how you plan to plan?

Fortunately we don't have to reinvent the wheel. There's a whole discipline that's been devoted to discovering great ways to plan--the field of project management. We can take this field that has been developed to make everyone more efficient and productive in their day jobs, and apply it to our creative work. Then we can then hack at it until it works for us.

This can be yet another way these sometimes grey-beige profit machines called businesses can provide a base for the wide color range of joy and adventure we put out into the world.

BITE-SIZE ESTIMATING

This is something I feel very comfortable in saying as an absolute:

No one *ever* does an entire thing at once. Every big thing ever done was done one step at a time. Even spontaneous songs, short stories, sculptures, impromptu sets – they all were done one part at time. Just in what was most likely a glorious fun flow. (More about the flow experience in the next section.)

I also don't find it useful to wait until inspiration. Inspiration is wonderful and I love it. And also, a lot of the work doesn't need inspiration. That work can be done at any time available--which frees us up *for when* inspiration happens. It also can lead *directly to* inspiration. When what's right in front of us is completed, the way is clear for new connections and directions to come before us.

I take some things to heart that Stephen King has said:

Sometimes you have to go on when you don't feel like it, and sometimes you're doing good work when it feels like all you're managing is to shovel shit from a sitting position.

In all of this, there are no absolutes. Sometimes you simply can't bear to do a particular creative thing one bit more. You know you have to try something else.

In those cases, I definitely suggest switching to a different creative project--*not* stopping entirely. It's important to recognize when frustration is part of a particular project, and not drive ourselves into the ground on that project so much that we associate creativity itself with that level of pain.

In my life it has worked very well for me to always err on the side of doing something. So I feel safe in suggesting you try the same. I'd expect you'll have the same generally positive results.

A way to make doing creative things easier and more possible: break the creative endeavor down into smaller elements that you can more easily see the beginning and ending of. As the saying goes: how do you eat an elephant? One bite at a time.

A famous marathon runner was once asked, "How do you get out of bed and run 30 miles every morning?"

The runner answered, "If I ever got out of bed and didn't feel like running, I promised myself I only had to go to the corner. Once I got to the corner, nine times out of ten I figured I might as well keep going."

Figure out what you can do sustainably, and do that regularly as a minimum. Daily can be great, also weekly. I have found both daily and weekly sets of actions work well for me, even if I only wrote five new sentences that week. It can feel silly doing just that, but even that as a minimum is twofold in its effects:

1. It really does accumulate over time. And you will almost certainly find yourself writing more than that minimum sentence most days – it will likely snowball into paragraphs and pages, and then you're at a fast productive clip. And just one page a day is a 365 page draft a year.
2. Second, and really very important, it is reminding yourself daily that you are doing this. It is an affirmation by action. And if you miss a day, by the way, that's fine too.

If you mainly create music, painted art or some other creative endeavor, try adapting this outlook to that other media. I am very sure you will find yourself able to create more and I expect you will find yourself enjoying it.

KEYWORD: sustainable

Repeated small efforts over binging. When you can get a lot in, do it. But if you can't do it, don't worry about it. Just do what bit you can. Over time consistent production can easily outstrip the binge / exhaustion / healing cycle. And generally with more fun and joy too.

Of course if binge production works for you don't listen to me, go for it. :) And I do think it's worth just trying out from time to time. A fun example of what I mean by "binge production" is a challenge called National Novel Writing Month, or NaNoWriMo. For those who might not be familiar, it's a yearly challenge to create a novel from start to finish.

Yeah. It's absurd.

And their definition of what a "novel" means is playfully pragmatic perfection. A novel is 50,000 words that aren't necessarily the same words in a row.

That's it.

So out goes any need to have any worries about quality – which can be a real difficult starting point for a lot of people. It's all about quantity. Did you hit 50,000 words in a month? Congratulations, you are now a novelist. :) Did you not hit it? Ah well, you still almost certainly wrote more words than you would have otherwise – which is a real success all of its own and more important than attaining the (still fun) title of novelist.

And within that, consider that it is *almost impossible* for all of those 50,000 words to be bad. Even at random, and more likely because you freed up yourself and came across a fun vein to explore, *at least some part* of that 50,000 words will be new and lovely and of solid quality in its own right.

It's my opinion and experience that quantity *begets* quality. The more we write, the more we learn how to write and how to *have fun* in what we write. An award-winning competitive target pistol shooter once told me his Marine training included the saying "Everyone starts with about 2,000 bad shots. They just have to get through them." I wouldn't apply that exactly to writing but I like the model. Just writing helps you get through to what works. It's a hurdle similar to when I started playing guitar – it took about a year of practice for me to start enjoying what I was playing. When I did, the practice become more play and it fueled itself much more easily.

There are similar challenges for music (the RPM Challenge), painting (30 Paintings in 30 Days), design (here's an entire list of available challenges) and others. If those are your interests I recommend checking them out as well.

Take on an absurd marathon, and just revel in the sheer insanity of it.

Doing NaNoWriMo every year has taught me so much about what my actual limitations are – and how I can increase my capability and output with practice, like most any other sort of exercise.

But and also, my great takeaways have been how I can take what I learn to manage that month and apply it sustainably for the rest of the year. This has included practices that are now part of my regular creative production, including tracking, story prep and dictation.

ABOUT "DISCIPLINE"

"Discipline" above is in douche quotes not because I dislike it. I respect it very much and think it's a great concept.

I just think that a lot of people can treat discipline as if it's something they *don't have* and *must somehow get first* before they can start creating the things they want to do.

As a specific example, I have found a lot of people think that they need to have discipline in order to write, paint or make music every day. And they don't.

We don't need discipline to create every day. We just need to create every day.

And what's the one day we know best? It's not yesterday, and it's not tomorrow. It's today.

So create today. :)

And if it ends up that you didn't work and play on creating yesterday? That's fine. Shit happens. And you can create today.

ADJUSTING **goals**

A forced march is not good or sustainable, or productive, besides violating the key point: kindness and compassion to yourself.

Make it work by making it play.

Working forward and playing forward from what you can do almost certainly means you can expand that to a good and workable, playable pace.

As an example, let's take learning to play a musical instrument such as a guitar. Like acquiring any skill, learning to play a musical instrument has a built-in difficulty slope. You get over the first and biggest hump when your playing is smooth enough that it becomes its own reward. You enjoy your playing enough to propel you to play more by itself, which in turn helps you to learn new ways to express yourself and improve your expression.

This point can come quite early in your journey, and well before what one might consider minimum proficiency to play for others. It can start getting fun for us pretty soon after we scratch the surface.

There are different ways for us to approach building our skills until we reach that point. One way is to go about learning things that are part of the formally recognized path to expertise in that field. In guitar this could mean things like sight-reading, chord theory, scales, and increasingly challenging musical pieces. Another way could be to pick specific songs you really enjoy listening to, whether or not they're considered difficult or even good by others, and then learn them. A third way could be to learn the absolute basics and immediately start creating your own songs.

These are all ways we can gradually improve while enjoying the activity of learning. What matters most is that you find the path that is the most fun or you. Any way you take from that starting point will lead to greater familiarity and improvement, and the potential for more and further fun. And as you improve along these joyful paths, the more easily you plug into the joy of creating what you want to create.

When we do something that fascinates us from the start, it's much easier to complete the necessary basic learning that leads to increasing ease of expression. It's still difficult, but less so--because now your efforts are engaged in doing something that brings you joy. In fact the same amount of difficulty can now be pleasant--to be engaged in hard work at something that you're enjoying is inspiring.

6. PROJECT MANAGEMENT SPECIFICS

Project management methods

High level - clarifying all of the steps

These basic principles can help all creative endeavors.

- Make lists
- Take and save notes
- Figure out steps

Lists! Lists! All the lists!

Lists are handy here too. Yes, it's information that's already in your head. But again, when you write it down, it's out of your head and you can *see* it. You will most certainly have freed up space in your mind, and things will occur to that you haven't seen before because of it.

Let's take a specific creative example, such as you want to write a story. What does that entail?

For me that often means these choices, or very similar ones:

- book subject

- novel or novella
- characters?
- primary hero?
- primary villain?
- setting
- hero's goal
- villain's goal

Or let's say you want to publish a book. What does that mean? For me it usually looks like this:

- book draft stage: 1st draft
- edit
- review
- spellcheck
- critique
- integrate feedback
- Book draft stage: 2nd draft
- (repeat above)
- (research) find list of likely publishers OR
- (research) find out self-publishing steps

...etc.

Both of those are good as far as they go. What about the rest of your life? What does work need from you this week, this month? What does your life need from you?

Write that down. Make your to-do list for the day, the week, the month.

To reiterate another previous concept, I suggest doing this only to the degree that you need to and no further. Making lists can end up being a fine way to feel like you're doing things while not doing the main things. Actually doing the project can be daunting, and making the list to help doing the thing can become a way of avoiding starting because "the plan isn't ready yet".

The plan's there to help you make what you want – it's not a substitute for making it.

IDEA BANKING

Take and save notes on the ideas that occur to you. This works similarly to freeing up the mind by getting all the steps down. In this case you can have fun getting ideas down.

When an idea or a notion occurs that I find fun and/or just unusual, I write it down. Usually fairly soon after it occurs to me, right into my smartphone as an email to myself. I've gone to the level of having an email filter set up that will look for the text "story idea" in the subject line, and label it. This often frees up my mind to riff further on that idea, which I put in as a reply to that email. I can have fun threads that really explore an idea, which is just super fun by itself.

So when you have some minutes standing on a line, waiting for a bus or a ride, commuting, and you have an idea, record in text into your smartphone. Or a notepad, or similar.

You can audio record ideas too, which I find quite useful if I'm dropping off to sleep and fun things occur to me. Good friends haven't known I do this and have wondered if I'm nuts when I've stayed over their houses and they hear me in the middle of the night. But then I explain it to them and they understand me as their friend, the good nut they like.

TIME AND TIMING

Laying out the steps

We can often feel like laying out the steps is unnecessary work. Once it's done and we see how much time something might take, it can also feel daunting. Like anything else in this book, if it doesn't work for you then don't do it.

And also, like anything else in this book, I encourage you to first try it on.

List out all the steps, then figure out how much time you expect them to take, then add in the time you have available. Then record this, and when either the project is done or the time has passed, evaluate how accurate your initial estimate is.

Note that this process is not to make you feel bad. To the contrary, it is to help you feel good by helping you to get your process in sync with what you need to create. Including the essential resource of time.

Knowledge is power. Knowledge of the time and space it takes to create helps us focus and aim our power to create, and punch through the crap that might be in creation's way.

More specific tasks for laying out the steps can be:

1. List the likely steps for a project

For example, with an independently published book the steps could be: plotting, 1st draft, 2nd draft, external edit/critique, 3rd draft / integration of feedback, spellcheck, external edit, beta read, cover design, publish.

For a traditionally published book the last few can change. In that case the steps could be: plotting, 1st draft, 2nd draft, external edit/critique, 3rd draft / integration of feedback, spellcheck, submit to agents / publishers

2. Figure out how many hours each of those tasks might take.

For a book of about 200 pages, time how long it takes to write a first draft of a single page. Then multiply that by 200.

3. Figure out how many hours you have available to write in a week.

....That's how many weeks it's likely to take to complete that stage of this project.

Once you see that number it can seem stark, especially at first. I encourage you to take heart. The glass half full point of view is, if you move forward at that rate then it is virtually certain you can get that project done. Vagueness has been dispelled and a path has emerged. All it will take now is putting that time in.

I've found this especially useful when I'm at the halfway point of a writing project. Many times as I near the halfway point I'll feel the most doubt about its completion. I am furthest from each shore, the eager beginning point and the triumphant completion of the journey. Fortunately I can know how much more time it can be expected to take – and knowing that, I can have trust that if I keep plugging away I will get there.

DIFFERENCES IN TIME

The amount of time needed might be quite different for creating new art than for revising or finishing art. For example, I have found from tracking my production that first drafts can be a lot faster for me than editing. Times can also vary depending on time of year, external life events, the kind of project itself, and many other factors.

So, in addition to the many other ways to not beat yourself up, don't beat yourself up if something is taking more time than it "should", even if similar projects took less time previously.

Along these lines, it can be great and useful to leave yourself notes at the bottom of where you are pausing. This can be great for the initial production page too.

TIME MEASUREMENT AND PLANNING: *annual and quarterly*

At the start of every year, I split the new year into quarters and then months. Then I look at the next quarter first, and plan what I want to get done. Then I break that out further into each of the three available months. I make sure to include map out vacations, events, holidays, and weekends, including the rest and downtime I am likely to need. I work on this until I have a schedule that seems doable for the year.

And every year ends up being pretty different than that calendar for a lot of those months.

But in doing this over several years now, I'm getting better at estimating how much time a task will take. That time has shrunk too, which is heartening to be able to measure as it shows improvement in my skills. And when something invariably happens that *wasn't* planned, I already have some organization to my forces. I can then adjust my plan. And it's far easier to adjust a plan than to have to create one from scratch.

To paraphrase General-then-President Eisenhower, "No battle plan survives the first shot." Yet he still made plans. Why? Because when you have your forces organized and goals in place, you can more easily shift them to changing needs and new realizations.

Also and on another note: deadlines are magic. Whether or not you reach them they will increase your productivity. Be careful of using them as a cudgel to beat yourself of course – that's not what they're there for. They're there as things to aim for.

Then at the end of the year, look over the schedule and see how the plan changed. That will offer you a lot of very useful information about both what you want to do and what is good for you.

In closing, also schedule fun. And schedule time to be spent on nothing! You will end up being grateful for at least some time to idle and maybe even luxuriate in feeling bored.

5-YEAR AND 10-YEAR plans

Put it all in. How does your 1-year roll into your 5-year, and thus your 10-year?

At more expansive views details matter less of course. They will change. But put where you want to be in 5 years, and then start filling in the steps to get there. Those steps can now be *goals*.

And again, as always – this is not a way to beat yourself up. This is the kindness, compassion and love to invest time in yourself to plan out *what you want*. In a way that's doable and sustainable.

Things may take more time to do those things, they may take less. The point is to use your adult-world superpowers in a way to support the glorious, lovely child within you. Be the best possible world for the best possible employee, you, and set up your path.

SPECIFIC PROJECT MANAGEMENT **tools**

Agile

Agile is a method that's caught on in the software development world. Software development is a great place to look for advances in practical project management in general. There are a lot of different companies that are investing time, money and expertise in trying to do things faster and more effectively than any other companies. We can sit back and reap the rewards of their learning in our creative lives. It can be a nice way of knowing that, for example, Google is working for me.

The absolute barbaric basics of Agile, and I'm sure at least one project manager will gnash their teeth at this over-simplification, are:

- Take the project you're working on, and organize it into its discrete tasks. As simple as is useful, and no further. (Perhaps a familiar refrain by now.)
- Decide on a relatively short amount of repeatable time, called a "sprint". In software development these are often 1 or 2 weeks. These same time amounts can work well for creative work too, as they wrap usefully around weekends when there can tend to be more free time.
- Split those discrete tasks into 3 buckets:

1. things I can do this sprint.
2. things I can do in the immediate next sprint
3. backlog

- Get cracking on this sprint. :) If you finish this sprint's tasks before it ends, pull in something else from the next sprint or the backlog. If you don't finish all the tasks you expected this sprint, then no harm or foul. Just move it to the next sprint, or to the backlog.

Applying this to a concrete example, let's say you want to finish a first draft.

1. Figure out how many new pages you can write in a day. If you don't already have a ballpark for this number, set time and write for the next 2 days and pick that number. (Let's go with a hypothetical example: 2 pages a day).
2. Build out the sprint size. Let's say 1 week
3. Take a guess at how many pages it takes to have a novel. Let's say 200. Then estimate how many pages you can write in 1 hour of effort a day. Let's say 2 pages.

200 pages at 2 pages a day will take 100 days. Divide that 100 pages by 7 for the number of weeks this would take.

That would be 16 weeks, or 3 and a half months... and 16 sprints. BUT, that's also writing every single day and it's important to not burn yourself out either. So:

1. Budget in some free days. Let's say 2 for every week.They could be the weekend, or they could just be days during the week when you just relax after your day job. So at 14 weeks, that's another 28 days or four weeks.
2. Measure how progress is moving as you go along. If you find yourself not hitting your page count per day or per week, then readjust the metrics.

Remember, what completes projects is consistent persistence. Find what your pace actually is. Then go steady on that. It will gradually increase in time anyway--and more importantly it will be a sustainable and regular foundation.

We now have an allotted time for this project's first draft stage. It's 16 weeks, which is four months. This means we also have some basic expectations to aim for. This will hopefully help you feel better about not finishing a novel a week.

These metrics are all targets, not expectations. Some days will have more productivity while others will have none available. Some weeks will be easier than others. What matters more than binge productivity is just consistency.

Look at each sprint as an *iteration* – in software terms, a version that can be refined. You want to get the best model for what works sustainably for you in terms of production. This makes it much easier to know what you can do, and not be mad at yourself for having expectations of your own output that don't suit your practical realities.

The good part of this is also that your productivity can (and almost always will) gradually increase from what you find sustainable. Things get easier with doing, both in quantity and quality.

It may also be helpful to consider 1-month sprints on specific projects, or multiple projects in backlog and being pulled out as other projects are completed. National Novel Writing Month, which comes from engineers wanting to write, is something I find very useful.

Every little bit helps.

Pomodoro technique

This is a way to make the most of sessions and expand them, and find what works while training yourself to possible expand both the quantity and quality.

It gets its name from a kitchen timer shaped like a tomato that the method's creator used.

Basically, you work in smaller sprints when you sit down (stand, lie, float) to create. A good place to start is often 25 minutes writing, 5 minutes most specifically not writing – get up from the desk, walk around, get a drink of water. And then back to creating again. If at the end of 25 minutes you find yourself wanting to keep going, then do so until you feel complete. At that point, try another 5-minute break and then start another smaller sprint of 25.

This has been shown by studies to increase focus and output. I've also directly experienced it helping me train my brain to work longer. I've found myself extending the initial 25 minutes to regular 30, 40, or 50 minutes.

Interestingly, some studies claim that a generally perfect on/break exchange is exactly 52 minutes on and 17 off. I am skeptical with that much precision, as it does seem like an average to me. But it's certainly worth trying. I say give it a shot. Pomodoro technique

TRACKING

Like meditation, tracking can be annoyingly effective. Excuses can hide in vagueness. And I kinda like my excuses. I've put a lot of work into them. I want to see them fully in public, joke around with them, and have them out of the way of the production line.

Less whimsically, tracking can also affirm for me that I really am working quite hard and I am exactly where I should be - as well as show me where I might be able to free up more time.

And as a third benefit, the next time I embark on a project like this I can more accurately estimate how much time it might take. And as I often get faster at things in practice, I can be pleasantly surprised when this project is done earlier.

It also is useful for me track different phases, as they are not all the same. In writing, my first draft production is much easier and quicker than subsequent phases of revision. If I didn't separate these two, I would be comparing apples and oranges, to the detriment of my understanding of both phases.

Whenever and whatever I'm tracking, I'm also making sure to do it as a ballpark figure. Precision isn't needed, and past a certain point can be a distraction. The point of tracking is not precision data. The point is also not to punish myself for not hitting a goal, and thus hurt myself if I do make it or if I don't. The point of tracking is to a) estimate past results so I can plan out new projects, break them into bite-size chunks, and b) have a better understanding of what processes can actually work best for my creative and productive happiness.

WHERE YOU CREATE: in spaaaaaaaaaaaaaaace
Now that we've discussed finding and making time to create, let's discuss space.

After all, you need to do it somewhere right?

I found one method very effective for making sure I had a place to create even when I was very busy in my life. I took a corner of my very small apartment and kept it clear of anything that *wasn't* writing. This helped remind me that I was taking this seriously. It became a refuge to go and write in. I felt encouraged to stay in it and create, because everything *not* my creative writing was outside it. While I was there creating was all I saw.

I also found and continue to find it useful to go and write around other people, such as a café where I'm writing this very sentence that I expect will make it into the final book.

It's all about what works, and not everything works all the time, and some things work at some times and not others. But it is almost always the case that *at least one thing* will work. And the more you experiment and look at what works, the more you will assemble your own creative toolset for what works...your own creative playset for what *plays*.

To return again to one the wisest lines in rock music: you can't always get what you want. But if you try sometimes, you just might find you get what you need.

Quoting from some other artists:

Point: "A woman must have money and a room of her own if she is to write fiction."
~ Virginia Woolf

Counterpoint: "Virginia Woolf's idea of a room of one's own has never been the place for middle- and working-class women. We work with interruptions."
~ Ananya Chatterjea

Zooming out of the differing contexts both of the above artists come from, and just looking from the perspective of someone trying to do things: I agree with both of these quotes.

If you can make a room to write in and you haven't tried it yet, go for it and make a room. Or a space. Or any dedicated location you know is yours. (And ditto regarding the money of course.)

And if you can't make a room yet, don't let that stop you. You are resourceful. You can find a way. *Start creating what you enjoy and want to create right now.*

PORTABLE SPACE

For a time when I was commuting and I found it hard to create at home, I was actually parking and writing in the back seat of my car. It was exactly what I needed: enclosed from noise, enclosed from interruption, my space and territory and no one else's. I took a laptop and had a grand time.

Along those lines, a laptop is a great tool for most any creative art and not just writers. A tablet will also do in a pinch. Get yourself one and keep it yours.

VIRTUAL SPACE

And also, most everyone is able to have some level of smartphone. Even free ones provide a level of functionality that lead to incredible possibilities. You can at least generate and do draft work on creative projects, not just writing. There are music editing apps, visual art apps, and more. As one friend of mine has done, you can edit documents using phone dictation while rocking your baby to sleep.

For writing, a Bluetooth keyboard can work wonders. You can just sync it to your phone and start typing text into any number of different apps with many features, free and cheap, and then work on them more later on a computer.

Notebooks are also great too. I rode the subway for years and always brought a paper sketchbook and a pen to jot down thoughts and puzzle out concepts. I needn't be worried anyone was going to come by and nab it like I might be concerned about with a smartphone. They probably couldn't read my handwriting if they did.

7. OTHER HUMANS

Assemble your team

As you play in your creative realm you will start to come across things that help writing, which can take away time from writing itself. It will be great if you could do all of these things *and* write, but time is finite.

I'm personally of the opinion that whatever being(s) may have created everything set up time so that us aware bits of the universe would have to make choices. It makes life happen. Regardless of the ultimate reason we have finite time, it does mean prioritizing when we can and getting help with the larger tasks that help our writing flourish.

For example, if you can edit a book in 3 months but you can find someone who will do a fine job in 2 weeks, and you can afford it – do that. Similar for Photoshop cover mock-ups, if you're an indie writer like me. I recently saved weeks on a photo book I'm putting together by paying Rev.com $70 to transcribe 70 minutes of audio. Sure, I could have done transcribed it myself. But I might not have gotten to it for a long time, and that project would languish. I spent some diner money instead and ate in for a week, which was healthier for me too.

This is exactly the same for tasks in other creative fields. If you can find someone who can mix or edit your song and get a sound you can get in 5 hours but takes them 30 minutes, and you can afford it, spend that money. If you're a painter and someone can put together a flyer or a website that would take you 8 hours of your free time and could take them 45 minutes--or even if it takes them 8 hours that *you* can now use for painting, and you can afford it, do that. This is one of the best possible uses of that day job money you make.

I strongly encourage you to find and assemble that team of people who can do specific things for you. They often are not your friends at the start. If some are your friends before working and playing with you on creative projects, make sure that your friendship stays strong and healthy. Just as it would be with most day job relationships, keep that friendship free and separate from whether or not they help your creative work. This is both honest and healthy to your friendship, and best for your creative work.

After all, the people we like and love don't exist to do things for us (or we for them). If anyone is helping you out through their sheer affection for you, and especially if they're not being directly materially compensated, take extra care not to wear them out. Make sure to take hints and not overload them, and make very sure they know how much you appreciate all they do and who they are.

Collaboration

Sometimes making art can be lonely. Sometimes someone else's creative perspective can complement your own. Sometimes two or more people can come together to create something truly special.

Some art forms, such as acting, movie making and live performances, are difficult to impossible without others' help. And even such solitary pursuits as writing or painting can often benefit from sharing the work and play.

On the other side of it, just like all human matters, other people who can help us all make things wonderful can also introduce new layers of complexity and difficulty.

Your mileage, shared and your own, will always vary. Here are some principles that have helped me out in my collaborations, both when they worked and in figuring out why they did not.

SOMETIMES IT JUST DOESN'T WORK, AND *that's ok.*

Sometimes people are great artistic collaborators for us, and sometimes they aren't. If you're trying to collaborate with someone but they're not providing what you need artistically, then talking about that can be hard and awkward. It will ultimately be better for you both. It needn't be a value judgement. A lot of times tastes and goals just differ.

IT CAN'T ALWAYS BE *you pushing it*

Just like a romantic relationship, it's not healthy if all forward motion depends on you. If it seems like if you stop trying to push things forward then no one else will pick up the slack, it might be time to reconsider this collaboration.

WHOSE IDEAS HAPPEN?

Work out the territory fairly clearly from the start. If you all want different ideas and some of them won't work with others, which will get chosen to move forward? You can't win every conflict, or it's not a collaboration. You can't lose every conflict either, or it's definitely not a collaboration and you're working solely to fulfill someone else's vision.

ARTISTIC DICTATORSHIPS *vs. representative democracy*

In groups of more than two people, such as many bands, large mural projects, group art shows, movie making, etc. it will be rare that everyone will enthusiastically sign on to every idea.

One solution is to have default dictator who makes all such calls. To be clear, this is *absolutely fine* for art purposes. As long as people know this will be the situation from the outset, and they are free to leave any time they want, this is perfectly valid and in fact the working situation of many successful and decent artists and the artists who worked with them. This ranges from Prince to David Bowie to the choreographer Bob Fosse.

If the vision is more collaborative, that is fine too. This can call for a different way of working. Artists who would rather be less dictatorial in their vision can often go too far in the other direction, and try to get every person to enthusiastically love their idea before the group proceeds. It can be hard to get any number of humans to agree on anything, let alone something as unique as a creative idea.

So, rather than try to get everyone's buy in on an idea, concept or vision from the start, it can often be useful to break off with one or two memories and work out an idea. Then present this idea as something that a good case can be made for, to the rest of the group. If people want to change specific aspects of the idea, they can then join the people working on that idea.

This is essentially representative democracy.

WHAT IF MY ideas aren't gone with?

Like any good relationship, it's often not about avoiding fighting. It's about *how* you fight. Or more precisely, how you acknowledge, get into and resolve conflict.

I think, especially with collaborations of more than two people, it's good to fight passionately for your ideas--and then if other people don't agree, move on. If it's a long-term project or a long-term collaboration, then most likely in a few weeks the issue won't even be remembered.

WHAT IF YOU change your mind?

Good relationships including collaborations are based on honesty--with others and with ourselves. So, with the same beautiful brutality of romantic relationships, if you OR someone else can't work with someone any more, that's it. It's not a decision to be made lightly, but if it needs to be made, make it. And if someone else makes it, respect it. You don't have to like it, and they don't have to like your choice either. But in all healthy relationships and especially creative ones, honesty is the irreplaceable bedrock for every other thing of value.

Not all people have the right temperament to collaborate with you

Not everyone can get along and work long term with everyone else, and people pursuing art are no exception. Sometimes people can even be great at collaborating with others, but their style just doesn't work with you. No harm no foul. If it doesn't work it simply doesn't work.

Collaborating with friends

Similarly, collaborating with a friend is beautiful and can be very difficult. I happen to be very good at collaboration with a lot of people who have a wide range of backgrounds, experience and temperaments. And even with this, there are some great friends of mine who are also truly excellent creative artists, who I have found I just can't work with.

Which is fine. I have other great and lovely friends who I don't travel well with, and have made poor matches as roommates. I still love them. We don't have to be good at doing all things together.

Collaborating with friends level 2: business

When you can work with friends creatively, and you find yourself working on a project that could make a lot of money, is taking a lot of investment of money and time, or both, it is very important to be clear what decisions are coming from what aspect of the relationship.

Friendship is friendship and business is business. Business requires clear boundaries and agreements. It can feel uncomfortable to get such clear boundaries with someone we care about; we can feel we "shouldn't have to nail down every detail." But friendships are also more likely to suffer from vague boundaries than firmly stated ones. Memory is fickle, and if the agreement isn't nailed down it's easy for *both* sides of it to remember it differently. This is just a consequence of how the brain works. We tend to place memories in a narrative and that narrative stars us as the central character, so it's naturally easy for that narrative to shift so we look great to ourselves.

If you're going into a creative venture with a friend that seems like it might make a lot of money, or cost a lot of money and time, or both, do everyone a favor and just set out the basic expectations in a document and kick it around until you both like it. Then email each other a copy.

It is so much easier for someone else to know someone else is keeping their word, and have them know you are keeping your word to them, if all the needed words are already agreed on.

Support

It would be great if we can depend on support from our family and loved ones. Sometimes we can't.

If someone you love or who is at least in your life a lot is supportive and helpful to *how you feel* about creating, and what you want to create, then share with them as much as you want.

If someone you care about or is in your life is *not* supportive and does *not* make you feel good, whether towards what you're making or just in general, then - regardless of how "constructive" they may think their criticisms are – I *firmly* suggest you don't share your creative process or efforts with them.

You don't have to. Why should you? Family obligation? Fuck that.

There may be other things you have to do. This is not that. This is one reason why pseudonyms were created. They don't ever have to know, and it's their loss. Your creative heart comes first.

Separately, some people in your circle might wish well and be very *emotionally* supportive – they just won't help you with *production*.

I am blessed to have great, kind and generous friends. They have given me a sympathetic ear when I needed it, and more. They have loaned me money, they have helped me move. They would probably hide me from the cops, and still some of them simply *will not* read a story of mine and let me know how they liked it.

And that's perfect and fine. We're friends because of all the important, lovely and fruitful ways that we relate. Helping me out with some of my specific creative production needs isn't any required part of that.

PEOPLE WHO MIGHT NOT UNDERSTAND **your creative needs**

Some people are really loving and supporting, they just live conceptually in the box. And ideas, proposals and actions which are new to them and/or out of the box are seen as dangerous just by having those qualities alone.

And creating is often out of the box, or working as if there is no box and going wherever it likes. This can be very threatening to people in and of itself. These people often otherwise offer no ill will and are even supporting and loving – just not to your creativity or the results of it. They just don't understand and are even threatened by things that contrast with the borders of their box.

Some people can even be loving and supporting in general, but just can't get their heads around creating and creativity as you see it. And they end up being a "no" just from who they are. Asking questions that amount to asking you to justify your passion to them, like "Why would you do that?" As opposed to coming at your passions with a more positive perspective of "Why not do what you enjoy?" Or "There must be a way you can do more of that. Let's brainstorm." Or even the automatically assumed "that sounds fun."

Non-partners

If these are not people you're currently building a life with, then I suggest: head this off at the pass. If they're tending to make pursuing your creative passions difficult, then there's no need to discuss this with them. It's not their business.

We don't have to involve them in our creative work. They don't need to know about it. We don't need to waste the time and energy and effort to answer their questioning, even if (as is very likely) you have a reasonable answer for every question.

And if they still want to be involved but aren't being helpful, then it's time for work on our own boundaries. It behooves us to make as clear as we can that we are not going to discuss it with them, and if they care about us they'll stop criticizing and/or demanding that we justify the things we want to do.

Please note that this is entirely different from criticism that is at least intended as helpful. Such as "that way might be hard – here's a way that might be easier." Or "I love that kind of stuff! Here are some artists you might not have heard of who have great approaches to that."

Romantic and/or Life Partners

The concerns and differences of opinion from someone you are closely involved with, and maybe even building a life with, are another category. A close partner's "I don't know if you're going to be able to do that," whether coming from specific concerns or a more amorphous fear of the unpredictable, must be dealt with a different way.

Just as your feelings are yours, their feelings are theirs and none of the feelings themselves are wrong. They may have an entirely different way of looking at the world.

As one example, a good friend of mine who is helped review this manuscript related to me a situation with his wife. They love each other very much and find each other wonderful, but their outlooks on life are different. She spent the last 15 years of her life in dedicated study, and is utterly committed to her medical career. She can have a hard time understanding his creative urge to jump from project to project, especially when profit is not necessarily the deciding factor. It just goes against everything she's been taught all her life, as well as her own current frustrations including paying back all of that tuition.

So they talked it through and came to a great compromise. She leaves him his creativity, and he promises to see each creative project through to its end before he starts the next.

A loving partner can understand that your creativity is a key part of the rest of the person they love. With patience and exploration, you both can come at this and find a way everyone can win. It's reasonable for such a close partner to want to make sure that the whole situation is working. A lot of the comments they present may be things you've already considered, which can be annoying. But they are coming from a place of wanting to be of help and make things work. Help them help you both. Find a way to make things work with them.

AND THEN THERE'S **straight-up jerks**

As for those who feel a need to criticize your creativity itself, whether it's in putting you down in general or criticizing your every particular idea or plan until it passes their own muster, they should meet increasingly firm boundaries until they either get the point or get shown the door.

Their unwanted noses have no place in your personal creative business. And you have no obligation to tolerate them out of "civility", "politeness", "having a thick skin" or any other number of reasons. Your creativity needs no justification. You have no need to keep people around who demand you justify it to them.

GETTING **feedback on your art**

Getting feedback from people is useful, and I would say even vital. It can also be hard, especially when starting out in creative production. Getting and receiving useful feedback does get easier with practice. Here are some suggestions for speeding up the process of finding it and using it.

Enough people I know and respect have had enough hard experiences with some people they've come across, that I want to yell this from the rooftops:

You have no obligation to listen to anyone who is trying to make you feel bad.

If the feedback you're receiving from any particular person is shifting from the piece of art to *you*, and then going towards making *you* feel small, bad, wrong or in any other way negative *for any supposed reason* – put on the brakes right there. Tell them to stop.

If they don't stop, whether because it's "their" workshop or group or some other reason - then either they should leave or *you* leave. There is no value in "toughing it out". Why stay somewhere that someone is trying to hurt you or insult you? You're worth more than that, your time is worth more than that. If you paid money to attend where this is happening, then that sucks – but you won't make that money back by staying. That money's gone. If you are familiar with the fallacy of "sunk costs"–the money and/or time you've spent has become a sunk cost. In gambling terms, you've lost a bet at what you've found out is a crooked table. You will not make this experience worth it by staying there and continuing to take abuse.

It doesn't matter if the person giving the feedback is an excellent artist. They could even be your hero – but if they're making you feel small they *suck at giving feedback*. And most to the point they aren't helping you. They're hurting you, and you deserve better.

Don't allow them to hurt you. You have a duty to yourself and the world to protect the light you have. I don't care if the person in question is Beethoven plus Picasso times Charles Dickens. Anyone who wants to hurt your light can go fuck themselves.

I know of a writer who had her spirit so crushed in a writer's workshop by a famous author that she didn't write for years. The famous author has since died, and no one I know feels bad about their death.

KEEPING attacks distinct from passionate discussion

This is all separate from spirited discussion. People can get lively and contentious when digging into creative ideas, and it can be fun and beautiful for people to become passionate in their opinions. And as creative artists we want to keep our passions, they help drive us. Ideas, arts and passion are all subjective and lovely because they can feel like deep objective truths, even when they're not.

In discussion, people can say things that can be hard to hear, and can come across as unintentionally rough. And also, even in the most polite and considerate framing it can be hard to hear someone say critical comments about your creative work. A key distinction remains here: that the art is being critiqued, which is separate from you being put down, insulted and/or made to feel small.

With that distinction in place, it can be important to note that this useful and necessary criticism can still hurt. It's similar in a lot of ways to how hard it could be to hear someone say what they don't like about your baby. Nevertheless, the difference between your creative output and a human child, is that your creative output needs almost always needs feedback to grow.

So, when receiving feedback keep that in mind. Also, consider that at least 99.9% of the time those critiquing your work aren't intending to make you feel small. If and when someone's critiques do seem to be coming from a personal place, they often are on their own trip that has little to do with what you wrote or even you. This happens a lot more often in human interaction than people realize, me included.

None of that is any reason to be someone else's punching bag. Nope. Maintain your boundaries and make a point of stopping critiques that go past the work and start in on you.

(Award-winning author Mary Robinette Kowal has further useful information on taking and receiving critiques. This link is also in the "Further Resources" portion of this book.)

OTHER FEEDBACK CONSIDERATIONS

When you receive feedback that isn't just straight toxic, there are some things to consider. These are not reasons to *dismiss* feedback. Instead, these are some ways to have a clearer view of the *context* of the feedback, so you can weigh it according to its relevance to what you are creating.

Does the person giving the feedback:

- Create and play in the same field you are seeking feedback in?

If so,

- are they actively creating in that field right now?
- do you like their art?
- is their art currently released?
- if it is released, how is it being received?

If not,

- do they enjoy things in the same field and flavor as what you're creating? For example, if you're writing do the like the genre you're writing in? Do they like other authors in it?
- If they are not experienced with the genre, are they similar in other ways to your audience? For example, if you're writing a memoir that has a Somali character, are they Somali? If you're writing a romance, are they female? A teenage boy might not be the audience for your harlequin romance. (Then again, they might be. Just another thing to consider as you weigh their feedback.)
- What are their goals? If you're receiving feedback from a group of people, are there at least a couple of people whose goals match yours?
- Are they finishing things?
- Any feedback is great to start with. I think it's really valuable and important to be involved with people who are completing works and putting them out, and starting something new. These people are great productive

influences for me. Many people who are writing less can still be great writers and have valuable feedback. But I have yet to meet a writer who is producing regularly who lacks great and insightful feedback, even if I don't agree.

- How well do they receive feedback themselves?
- Are they open to discussion and can express reasonable disagreement? Do they try to get clarity on someone's opinions, rather than debate them?
- Alternately, if someone disagrees with them do they get brittle and defensive?

Sort and weigh their opinions accordingly. And always remember that you are the ultimate judge and God-ruler of what you want to do.

WHAT KIND **of feedback should you give?**

For the feedback you give others on their works, consider the inverse of the previous points. What do you have to say, and how might you say it, to help their own goals?

While giving your feedback, also consider what may be already clear but is well worth saying: you can't change someone's style as a writer or artist. They will write how they want to write, and they should write how they want to write. So your part of the equation is to try to give them the feedback that will help them towards doing what they want.

6.66 MONEY AND CREATIVITY

Money is a tough topic that can make a lot of people feel very weird, with me very much included. We live in a commerce-based society. At the same time, we have hearts and spirits and joys that don't connect with money at all.

I don't have any secrets for making money. If and when I do, you better believe I'll be writing that book. Instead, these are some general ways that I like to treat the topic of money for creative works, so that making money can also be a goal of mine without undermining my creativity, my good spirits or my fun.

For all of these reasons I like to treat money as a separate game. One I can play intensely, while also keeping clear that it's a separate game than my creativity.

If money isn't **a goal of yours, that's 100% okay.**

It's more than okay. It's so okay it doesn't ever need me or anyone else to declare that it's okay. It's not only okay, it's fine as in beautiful. It's as lovely as the wind, the sun, the moon and the rain.

I think a lot of creative people can make themselves sad by thinking they have to make money for their art or it isn't good enough. I think that's a crock. You make your art because it's beautiful to you.

MONEY ISN'T WINNING. **It's just some stuff.**

It can be considered really socially important to win, and money can often be used as a metric for who is 'winning.' This also implies that every person besides the single one making the most money in the world is 'losing.' So even people with incredible amounts of the money and fame they're supposed to want often aren't enjoying it at all. Rather than relax in relative freedom from material concerns, they live stressful lives where they still pursue "winning" as measured by money. It's actually impossible to keep winning that way. But they can feel like they have to keep trying, or they'll really start sinking behind and 'losing.'

And where's the fun in that?

Creating is fun. Creating is enriching. Even when we make things are sad or scary, haunting or upsetting, they fulfill a real purpose that is as perhaps as close to spiritual as we can directly see on Earth. Our creations connect us to ourselves, and in doing that connect us to each other.

Money is a side point in that whole game. You should be able to get together with people you know make a band and play songs and play out if you want or record at home if you want, or just play, without the stress of whether or not you're going to "make it". Write what you want to write. Paint what you want to paint. This creation itself is a gift that can't be sold, and which increases the more people you share it with.

With all of that said, the side game of making money can point to ways you can shape how you play, including how you communicate with people who might enjoy your creative art. And it can ultimately lead you to creating full time. Which is an ultimate goal for many of us artists. And that's fine too.

I just want to emphasize that whether or not you pursue making money with your creative passion, and whether or not you achieve that side game, your creative passion itself is *always* worth pursuing and is *always* more valuable than what your art might make sell for in the marketplace.

With all of the above in mind, here are some considerations on the creative side game of money.

CREATING to market

I have found it interesting to consider what I want to say, and what the market wants to hear. Not so I can speak falsely, but to find common ground. In the most honest sense of a marketplace of ideas, I want to say things I enjoy saying that others find useful and worth hearing in a way that pays me money.

I have found it useful to view these realms of my desire and market desire as a Venn diagram.

What I want to create, and what the market appears to be paying for is a circle that does or doesn't overlap.

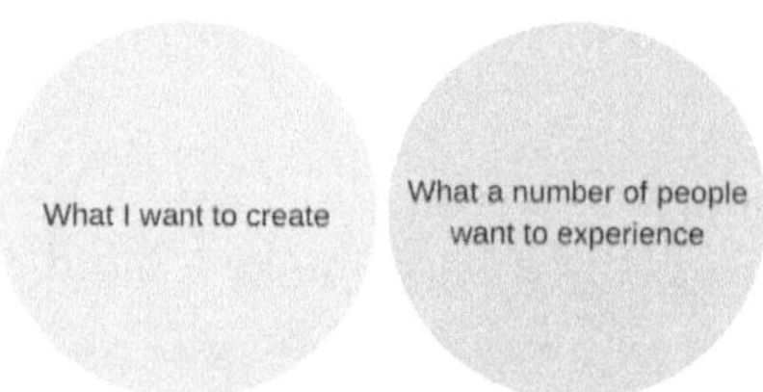

The question is, how might I expand what I like to write into what the market appears to be paying for?

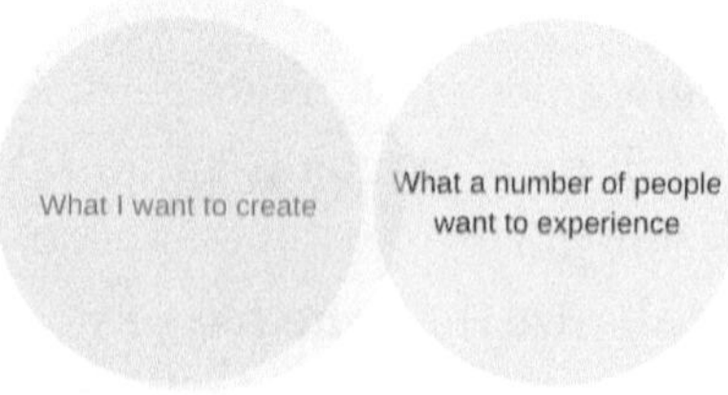

That can be a fun challenge. It's led me into writing cozy mysteries this year, which is outside of my previously creative play in science fiction and fantasy. The result has been a lot of fun for my overall writing – for once I don't have to worldbuild and explain unusual ideas and people's realistic reactions to bizarre things that haven't yet happened. I can just get into characters and what they're like, and how they bounce off each other.

"Creating to market" is essentially looking at what is currently selling like hotcakes, and taking at making that. Creating can also take a lot of time of course, so I wouldn't suggest starting to write a different kind or genre of store and continuing with it if you find you really *don't* like it. You might end up struggling with something and having the market move by the time you get it to press.

But it can be a useful way to stretch yourself and find new things about what you make and what others are making too.

ANOTHER CIRCLE: **what's physically possible**

In recognition of what's sustainable and treating ourselves with kindness and compassion, consider what's good for us physically. And how can we improve that?

This would be a third circle to draw in.

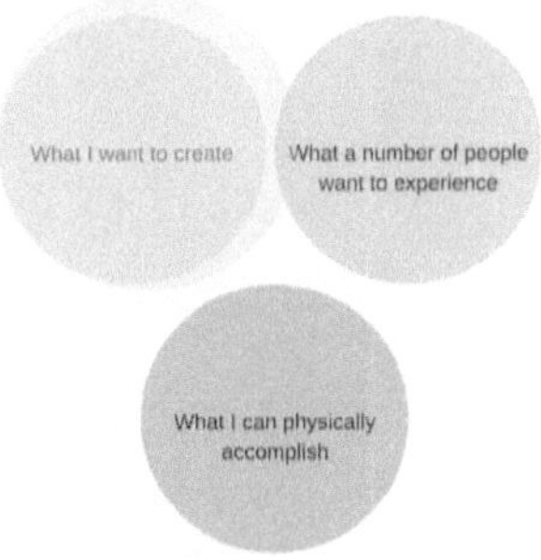

This can also be good in general for looking at comfort zones and how they might be expanded.

What do you need to expand?

Where is easiest to expand?

Where might be most productive to expand?

What are concrete steps you can take to expand them?

This circle can then be enlarged by possible exercise and other tools to help physical limits.

If you don't have a specific direction that occurs to you, then out of kindness, compassion and their pragmatic cousin sustainability consider expanding the sphere of what you enjoy creating. This will most certainly expand into the sphere of what people like experiencing, but that's less of a focus. What we really want is where all three of these circles can best intersect.

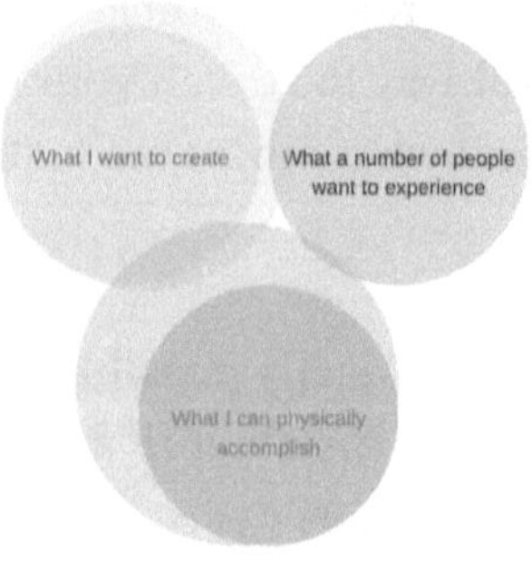

ONCE EXPANDING MORE THERE, we can start looking for the sweet spot:

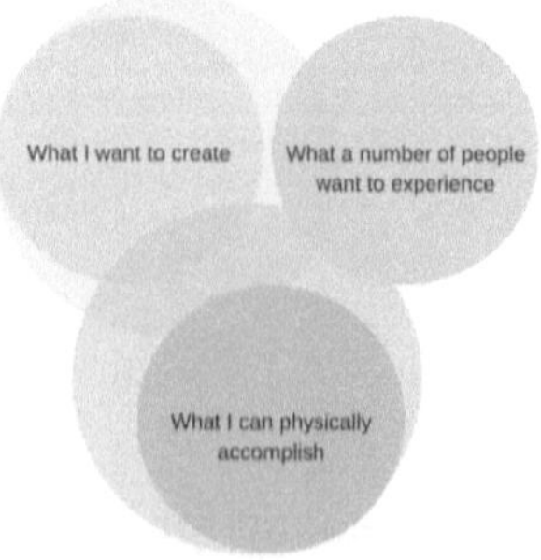

WHAT THIS EXTENDED Venn exploration means in practice: consider what you can expand that will help you out in all of these circles. With kindness and compassion for yourself ever in mind, you almost cannot help but expand your life.

As one example, a common problem that can affect writers' output is back issues. Tools to help us heal physically and enlarge this physical circle of the Venn diagram can include:

- a regular exercise program
- a standing desk. This needn't be a rising standing-sitting desk if that's too costly. A shelf can be built fairly easily out of lumber. This will enable you to write without having to sit down for long periods and strain your back.
- an ergonomic kneeling chair. A less expensive alternative can also be a sitting ball chair.
- a treadmill . Acceptable models can be found for $200 - I know, I've tried it. When combined with dictation and a standing desk, this can be a great combination for first draft writing.
- a stepper - even smaller, simpler and cheaper than a treadmill, this can be something you put beneath a standing platform

ADVERTISING

For the side game of money, it's good to become familiar with advertising. This can be especially useful if you're an independently published writer. This is treating your creative output as a small business. And pretty much every small business I've ever known has advertised. They have a specific budget for it. Humans are as we are, and there are a lot of things we can pay attention to.

As another aspect of this game, if you're playing as a small business then don't go too deep in the red. Make a good product, and start shopping it around. Spend a bit of money to see what your returns might be, as long as it's fun. I would not drop thousands at least until you're making hundreds, and I would not drop hundreds at least until your making tens. And in general, if what you're spending on advertising has you underwater compared to what you're selling, it is probably worth dropping those ads until you can figure out something else that will put you in the black.

Also, and back to the main game: the real answer to selling the current album, book, painting or other piece of art is often creating the *next* one. When people like one thing you've made, they often come back for something else.

So whatever else you do on the side game of money, make sure you are creating the next piece you want to create. And working on it until its completion.

SECTION TAKEAWAYS

In this section, we've come down from higher levels of abstraction to just above the trees in the forest. We've looked at different ways and methods we can work with the two most raw materials available to all artists, and really any humans embarking on any endeavor: space and time.

The methods we looked at for shaping these essential resources to our benefit include:

- Planning
- System design
- Copying from those you admire
- Experimentation
- Estimation

And we also looked at more tactical tools:

- Journaling
- List-making
- Note-taking
- Project management
- Time measurement

- Tracking
- Creating portable work spaces and environments

Finally we discussed the side game of making money from our creative works, and the importance of keeping it separate from our enjoyment of the main game.

Now we're ready to look into some very specific methods I've used, and I've seen others use, to increase both their writing output and their writing quality.

READY TO DIG into some more detailed ways?

Great! That's next.

CERTIFICATES

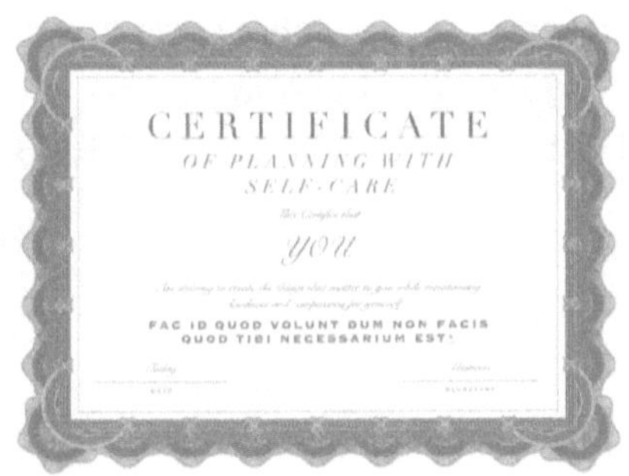

Permission Slip

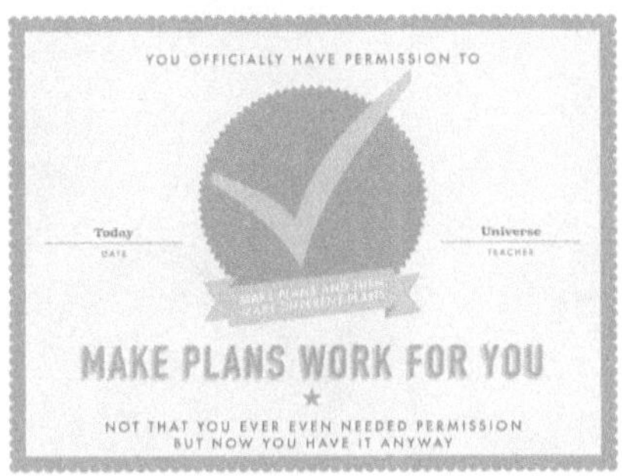

CREATIVE PRODUCTION

Now that we've gone into the view above the forest, and then zoomed in closer on the forest, let's get down to the tree level. What are some good ways to build in here, and what tools can help us build?

There are many ways to approach the crafting of writing, and specifically of story. Much of this next section is aimed at fiction writing, but the basic principles themselves apply very much to memoir, essays, and nonfiction such as even this book.

KEEP craft in context

When we're engaged in creating, and when we're thinking about creating, we're often trying to understand and reverse engineer general principles around the art that we like. We're often look for concepts that can help us generate more of the art that we like. Often it can be as much about trying to not do things we don't want as we're trying to do more things that we do. All of it;s in service to art that achieves the effect we want on others. That's one of the strongest purposes of art: communication, even if it's with ourselves.

So within the craft that comes with creating art, I can think of it as having two companies: how and why. The "how" is generally the science, and the "why" is often the magic. To take an example from popular music, and the Jimi Hendrix live take of his song "Machine Gun." The how is how he played--scales and chords, amps and electronic effects, the use of vocal emphasis, the use of beats per minute and rhythm.

The "why" is beautiful and mysterious. It's aided by all of the above, but none of that gets to why that song hits me so hard. Why, in the middle of that completely eerie solo, I get chills up my spine because I feel like I can hear him going over to the other side of the veil.

My point: the science is in service of the art. But it's not the art. The science is a means to an end: magic.

So if you are frustrated with your current level of ability in doing what you want to do, that means you are a craftsperson who cares. And that's to your credit. And developing your craft to any degree you want will improve your ability to make art that matters to you and others. It will give you more and better tools.

But the tools are less important than you. You are where the magic and the art comes from.

Moving towards completion

Moving forward

If you are trying a lot of the higher level methods already listed in this book, and still find yourself not moving forward on a story, here are some specific tactics.

To go back to the example from the Motivaction (™) * chapter earlier in this book:

"ABC: – Always Be Completing!" Always be taking some idea or project forward to complete it and share it with the world. And then on to the next one.

(* still not actually copyrighted)

Write the piece straight through to the end

This is just as barbaric and hardcore as it sounds: simply keep writing until you have reached the end of the story. Maybe let yourself read enough of what you previously wrote to know where to pick up again – but no editing. It can be useful to not even correct a single typo or grammatical error. Just and only keep going forward until you have reached the end.

This can be useful in a few ways. One of the largest personal benefits of this for me, was that writing all the way to the end taught me so much about what I needed the rest of the book *before the ending* to do.

This was also a very good way for me to learn to keep two mind-sets separate – creating and revising. People can get very locked up when they are doing both at the same time. Both mindsets are useful and beneficial, they are just often at cross purposes. So it can be good training, especially at first, to get used to doing mostly one or the other exclusively at a given time.

But to the main point, finishing a story will tell you more about writing than you will ever learn perfectly shaping the earlier parts of a story.

It also feels great. It also helps guard against other things that I've seen such as writers working so long on a story that they are weaving new ideas into it just to work with new ideas. It can be easier to explore those new ideas in new works.

As they say in software, it's good enough – ship it.

If you really want to force yourself to keep writing through the power of fear, there's a website called Write or Die. Thankfully, it won't actually kill anyone. Instead it works like this: if you aren't writing the next words fast enough, it will start giving you warnings. Then it will start deleting the last words you wrote. On the screen, right in front of you.

Less stressfully, some friends of mine have gotten quite good results from acquiring and setting up an old AlphaSmart. These machines from the early stone age of computers are basically type-writers with a digital window, where you can only see a few sentences at a time. When you're done writing for the day, you download what you've written. They're usually found quite easily on Ebay for roughly $20 plus shipping. If you do try out a Smart-Writer, make sure you also get the specialized digital cable to download the content. This device actually predates USB connections.

ALTERNATE TACTIC IF STUCK: consider other scenes or characters in the same story

If one scene is giving you trouble, maybe write two or three scenes after it and come back to it. You might have all you need.

ALTERNATE TACTIC IF STUCK: jump around

Start writing scenes or parts that seem fun. When you have all of those scenes, consider what the minimum number of scenes will be needed to fit them together. It might turn out that one scene you had a difficult time getting started on, or a part of the story you were unsure how to approach, actually wasn't needed at all.

In fact, many writers have found that if you just write the scenes that seem like the most fun first, you might need a lot fewer connecting scenes or setup than you might otherwise think.

ALTERNATE TACTIC IF STUCK: write a short story with one character

It can often be useful to just create a quick story with only one of your story's current characters, to get a feel for who they are. This can be a story that leads to the events your writing about elsewhere, it can be from a formative moment in that character's history, or it can be something else entirely.

SHORTER PIECES CAN BE great to write in general

Story is story. At a high level, arcs can have the same basic shape whether they are 500 words or 500,000. So short stories can be great laboratories to work with how all the elements that you want to have in stories work. You can take this on before you embark on longer journeys of words, and as quick larks in between.

. . .

PANTSING and Plotting

There are many different ways to go forward in completing a written work. A usual way to separate methods at a high level is the spectrum of "Plotters" vs "Pantsers".

Pantsers, as the name implies, write by the "seat of their pants." No preplanned plot, maybe not even an end goal, maybe not even characters. The root term "flying by the seat of their pants" is worth looking into here. The phrase comes from the early days of human flight, when people would find their way to destinations with only the most rudimentary navigation equipment--or none at all.

Plotters, as their name implies, come from the other side of the spectrum. They intentionally plot and plan out what they are writing, with the hope that this will bring them close to where they wanted.

A SPECIFIC PANTSING TACTIC: writing into the dark

For pantsing, the method I've heard that has most intrigued me has been "writing into the dark". As described by very accomplished and almost absurdly productive writer Dean Wesley Smith. To summarize and perhaps unfairly bastardize it: he starts with an idea and some characters and writes forward until he runs out of steam. Then he goes back and cleans up the prose until his prior stopping point. Smith says that by the time he reaches where he had left of writing new text, he will always have new ideas that occur to him for what next might happen in the story.

As he's writing full time he's able to do this for several hours a day, ending up with thousands of words of pretty clean prose that needs minimal rewrites. This has enabled him to put out *several* novels a year for decades now. Working a day job, one might find less continuous blocks of time. But this still has its benefits, including continuous relative forward mention with pretty clean copy.

The analogy for "writing into the dark" is driving at night. You don't need lights illuminating the whole way. You only need to see the stretch of road that the headlights light up before you.

Stephen King appears to write similarly. He has said he makes sure to complete 1,000 to 1,500 clean words a day. Which could mean up to 6 novels a year. It's also worth noting that he hands them off to editors.

I related this daily number of King's to a fellow writer. Her response, which I loved: "Well then Stephen King can go fuck himself."

It always remains about what works for you. These are presented as inspirations and possible methods for you to experiment with in your own process.

SPECIFIC PLOTTING **tactics**

I tried plotting so much at first, and it didn't work for me. I found it very frustrating, I would work out an extensive roadmap and then the characters or aspects of the story I hadn't considered because I didn't have my hands in the guts yet would take me far and wide away. And I certainly wouldn't want to junk a fun idea or escapade because it didn't fit the plot. You don't ditch the free car because it's parked sideways. Or whatever other analogy you prefer.

I tried 3-arc sketches for a while, but I found them too vague and not really helpful. Better than nothing, but a similar thing for me.

Long story short I came across these basic methods which have just worked great for me since then.

THE STORY before the story

This is a basic concept from mystery novel writing. Basically, what had to happen before the story in order to set up the events for this one? In a mystery, what series of events led to someone committing the murder that the actual story will investigate? Including how the murderer covers it up, and why, and what other character will then go on pull in the investigator.

Plot that out for your story, whether or not it's a mystery. It doesn't have to be something extensive. Whatever works for you, a page or less often works for me. Just have it be a plot with characters, events, arcs and probably even a surprise at the end, that leads to the inciting incident in your story.

I then plug this into one of my favorite writing tools I've found yet: Dan Harmon's Story Circle.

DAN HARMON'S *Story Circle*

Dan Harmon has gone from relative nowhere to becoming one of my biggest writing heroes. He is cantankerous and occasionally quite difficult, and has written some great shows. First "Community" and then "Rick and Morty". The latter is a great show in spite of what can be a very obnoxious fanbase.

Most to the point, I tried what he suggested and it has worked great for me. His method is called the Story Circle. It's a reconfiguring of the Joseph Campbell 'Power of Myth' story arcs popularized by Campbell himself, and lent a big hand to fame by George Lucas' use of this in the original 1977 Star Wars.

Basically, you have the protagonist goes through a series of steps like this and map the changes at every step.

1. **Status Quo**–where the protagonist starts
2. **Need**–the protagonist is introduced to a need
3. **Go**–the protagonist must leave their familiar surroundings to be able to fulfill that need
4. **Search**–the protagonist must search for a way to fulfill that need
5. **Find**–the protagonist finds a way they could fulfill that need
6. **Take**–the protagonist must pay a price to take what will fulfill that need
7. **Return**–the protagonist returns full circle, either in place

or in a situation, with what they have needed. A final conflict ensues based on that need.

8. **The Change**–we see the results of the return of that conflict and how it's outcome changes the protagonist and perhaps the world forever.

I've gotten great benefits from applying this method to planning before writing new stories, and also using it as a lens to diagnose previous stories that felt stuck. I highly recommend trying it out.

LESTER DENT's pulp rules

They are fucking barbaric and I love them.

1. Start with a hero under a cloud.
2. Have a villain with a unique way to kill people
3. Have a physical conflict every 1500 words
4. End with either a clear total success for the hero or a clear total failure.

In parallel with this, legendary mystery novelist Raymond Chandler said "When in doubt have a man come through a door with a gun in his hand."

CHARACTERIZATION

After a long search where I wasn't fully sure what I was looking for, I finally found a book that gave me what I needed re: characterization. Essentially a simple process to make sure I wasn't missing things. The book itself is Story Flash by Alexander Astremsky. The basic steps as I've adapted them, below. I've also found working through this in a spreadsheet program to be quite effective.

1. Pick the protagonist, the antagonist, a protagonist's helper and an antagonist's helper.

2. Describe the protagonist and the antagonist.
3. what do they each want to achieve?
4. what do they each want to avoid?
5. What method do each of them use to try and achieve their intentions?
6. What are their skills, knowledge and abilities?
7. Drill into the protagonist
8. What are the protagonist's tools?
9. What is the protagonist's emotional wound?
10. How does it affect his personality and actions?
11. What is his flaw (for example, does she have a bad temper? Is he naive?)
12. Drill into the antagonist
13. what are their precise goals?
14. What do they think those goals will help them achieve?
15. what do they want to avoid?
16. what makes them so invincible, unpredictable and talented?
17. Reason for confrontation
18. what is the main conflict?
19. why does protagonist oppose the antagonist?
20. why do they resist each other so furiously
21. How does the antagonist make things difficult for the protagonist--what barriers do they create?
22. Antipathy towards the antagonist
23. Describe the negative actions taken by the antagonist
24. Specify why these actions will make the audience dislike them
25. Secondary characters

Go back to the friends of the protagonist, and describe their intentions and goals, the strong points of these characters, their weak points and so on. If you will be working with characters and are at all curious I highly recommend this book. Filling out a list like that, and other lists like them, can seem like a lot of typing. :) But when I've used this, both in first drafts and in diagnosing story issues during edits, it has saved me a lot of time.

Using a list like this does not in any way make us beholden to it. We can change our mind at any time in writing. Just having considered these areas helps me have a rich vein of opportunities to choose from. I don't have to figure out new things from scratch while I'm trying to produce words--so I have more mind to spare for the words themselves.

COMBINING **the two for plantsing**

Yes, this is a thing. As the word suggests, "planting" is a combination of plotting and pantsing. Many writers find themselves in this space after a while–planning out some portion of the story ahead of time, and then letting the words fall where they may. For example, one writer I know will have a basic sheet of paper that he'll note very high-level considerations on and keep it next to his laptop while he bangs it out. This is very technically plotting, even though his daily writing would be pantsing.

IN THIS, as always, what is most important is what helps you create and produce to your greatest joy.

Output

Wordcount expansion

WE DON'T JUST HAVE to always produce words at the same speed. We can expand those words while keeping the same level of quality -- and we can often increase both the quantity and quality.

NaNoWriMo

As mentioned previously, National Novel Writing Month AKA NaNoWriMo can be a great way to blow the doors open and put down words. I strongly suggest going for it at least once, if not every year for the rest of your life. It also doesn't have to only happen in November. I frequently jump in on at least one of their other marathons throughout the year.

SHUT *Up and Write*

Similar to the spirit of NaNoWriMo, Shut Up and Write is just what it sounds like. A group of writers agree to meet up at a specific area, get a table, and write. They have groups meeting regularly in over 230 cities around the world.

THERE IS something about writing in community that can really make words happen. It might be as simple as fully realizing we as writers are not alone.

WRITING TACTICS PART ~~DEUX~~ 2: Rewriting

There may be some writers who are happy with what their first draft without any further rewriting, and without even going over their first words once. If so, I salute them. There is no one I know personally or have heard of who does not rewrite to some degree.

Even the famed Beat writers of the 1950s who prized spontaneity would edit. Jack Kerouac would strike out entire sections of stream-of-consciousness text that he found off-point. William S. Burroughs' difficult and brilliant Naked Lunch was selected and reassembled from pages written in stream of consciousness.

And that's for people who preferred not to edit. Most writers, including me, require much more editing and rewriting than the Beats to produce our works.

I've found that I can pre-emptively reduce the amount rewriting I'll need with:

- Worldbuilding
- Having the simplest plot you need (but not simpler)
- Evaluating how you are treating that plot. The general spectrum is one side treating the plot as a guide that can be wandered from, and on the other side a firm requirement that must be stuck to no matter what.
- having a clear villain, a clear protagonist, a clear setting, a clear threat to the protagonist, and opposed objectives for the villain the protagonist at the start

That said, this is coming from my own typical ways I approach a new story. I can tend to have an overall idea, consider a possible to likely end, and then have a conflict that leads to a plot laying out the journey to middle. Then when new ideas occur if they seem even more juicy and fun I go with them.

So if you don't want to listen to me, don't :) Do it your way always.

I do suggest you write at least a few stories that hew directly to basic principles of introducing a clear protagonist, antagonist, setting, threat to protagonist and conflict before dropping one or all of them. It's not that you shouldn't break these or any other 'rules'–I'm a firm believer in you creating whatever you want however you like. It's just that these are ways to put power into a story. It can be beneficial to understand through practice how these principles work, and what power they introduce.

This way if you make a conscious decision to ignore a particular rule, you can make an informed decision about what power you might be giving up. Then you can come up with ways to adjust the overall writing in other ways and increase the impact on the reader.

As a specific example of this, let's say that you want the reader to not be sure what the story setting is. At the same tine you're also having the character be an unreliable narrator who may or may not be hallucinating at any given time. You also want the reader to be experiencing this subjectively, from the viewpoint of the character.

If you are familiar with these principles in practice, then you can have a feel for how these choices might make it harder on the roader.

So you will know that if you want to keep the reader's interest, with less clarity in setting or protagonist you will probably have to make the conflict more clear and the character more appealing and sympathetic. This can grip the reader in other ways, while still maintaining your artistic intent. And probably even amplifying it.

SIDE NOTE: **Kill your darlings (only metaphorical, does not include actual living darlings)**

If you find a scene is not working, even if you love it consider removing it from the story. Just save a new draft if needed, and in that new draft cut that scene out and keep rewriting.

This is hard advice that comes directly from the excellent writer Joss Whedon – and it can be very useful and helpful. You can put the scene back in later if you want – you will just most likely have a more full understanding of what the overall story needs and how that scene can help it or how it might have to be altered to provide it.

REVIEWING **and iteration**

Whatever method or combination of plotting/pantsing/plantsing you pursue, once you have reached the end of your first draft it might be worth looking at your plot or your original starting point. This is a good way to see how your methods have worked, so you might make adjustments to your process for your *next* work.

If you're looking at plotting, how close was your original plot to what ended up? As an example, in my most recent mix of plotting and pantsing methods, I found myself having to add in a lot of details to the plot while I wrote.

Is this a sign that I need to do my initial plotting at a higher level of detail? It could be. Of course it could also be that thanks to my initial plot I could more easily create subplots on the fly--and maybe I should leave room for that, so the story can develop flexibly around the main thread.

If you're pantsing, how much rewriting might now be needed?

Maybe none, in which case kudos! If not, that's hardly a failing. Rewriting can not only help the current work, it can show ways to adjust your process for the *next* work.

There will always be more to learn and work on. This is about upping our game, while having fun with it as a game.

FEEDBACK FOR WRITERS

Critique Groups

We have to know how the words from our heads play for others outside our heads. Critique groups can be very useful for this. Also, like dealing with humans in any capacity, they can become complicated and difficult. I've found a lot of this complication can be sorted through with a few basic principles. Some of these principles were discussed in more detail in the previous section "Getting feedback on your art."

1. Treating critique groups as focus groups

I find it useful to treat critique groups less as ways to gather advice and more as focus groups. Sometimes those in it can offer great advice. Other times that advice might not work at all, but the people who give it can still feel quite attached to it. But whether or not I agree or even like the advice, the opinions and places they're coming from are great information.

Like any focus group, understanding the person giving the feedback is key. Do you they like your genre? Are they familiar with your genre? Are they your intended audience?

2. Don't feel like you have to listen, and also don't just ignore them

You are under no obligation to listen to anything you don't agree with. And also, their opinion isn't wrong. This is an audience member responding to what you have created. If one person says something that completely surprises you, that might be just randomness. If a majority of the group says something reads a certain way that surprises you, it's more likely that you as the author didn't see it and might want to look at it again.

Similarly, it's not useful to argue with someone that they "should" understand something differently. A member of the audience didn't receive something in the way you intended. This is the feedback that you're there for, that you need to find out. Once you have this information, you can choose if it seems important enough to adjust to or not.

In general I've found it useful not to listen to people's advice necessarily, but to go a level deeper and look at *what they might be trying to solve*. If a bunch of people are trying to fix a particular set of paragraphs in your piece, look at that section again. Some part of that prose is a stumbling block. The reasons it isn't working might not be in that section at all. There could be something else several paragraphs earlier or later that works fine by itself, but is causing a contradiction. The main point to keep i mind is, something relating to the section that people are trying to solve is not having the effect that you intended.

Ultimately, if you can't change the passage or the piece so that this difficulty is resolved that's fine. And it's even more fine if you just don't want to. That's so beyond fine that I don't even need to say how fine it is. In cases like those, I suggest moving on through the rest of the piece to completion. Then one that piece is done enough, then move on to the next idea and the next new piece.

3. Make sure you get feedback that's useful

If it happens that you aren't getting the feedback you want at the moment, you can and probably should ask for it. People are often reacting rather than thinking forward.

It often helps to prime the pump. Spell out the kind of feedback you're looking for, *before* the crit group reads it.

"This is an early draft, so I'm mainly concerned with: are the characters relatable? How's the pacing? Does the background seem to logically make sense?"

"This is a later draft, so please let me know - is the ending satisfying?"

4. Use critique groups for critiquing, not proofreading

I've found it good to make sure I spellcheck and grammar check my piece before submitting it. Besides being considerate for them, it's good for me. If critiquing is getting bogged down in spelling and grammar edits, that's less time and effort spent on what critique groups are best for: how the piece itself might come across to readers.

You can often find critique groups in your area by searching in Meetup.com. There are also online critique groups such as Critters.org, which I have found quite useful.

Pro/paid editor feedback

All the above considerations apply in some regard. In addition:
-make sure the editor gets and likes your piece's genre
-listen to their feedback, and try it.
-when the story is fairly complete, ship it and start the next one.

Artificial Feedback

There are a number of good resources for tracking down those sentences and paragraphs that sounded fine in our heads, but didn't work nearly as well once typed. I've found ProWritingAid to be excellent. They generally offer seasonal sales for "lifetime subscriptions" (i.e. a one-time fee) as well as monthly access. Hemingway is free online and $20 for a desktop version. Edit Minion also offers fine options for tracking down lugubrious, turgid or plenitudinous prose.

Like spellchecking, these are key improvements that are worth applying at every stage. They will lead you to find other things to tighten up your prose at every point in the process.

Beta Readers

At a certain level of production and/or speed you might find that a critique group is not providing enough feedback for you. At this point, and also just for other readers, you may look into cultivating a group of beta readers.

Not necessarily your friends. If so, that's great. But what you're really looking for is people who *like* to read to say what is and isn't working for them. Their tastes should be aligned with yours, and they should be able to share their thoughts without it stressing either of you out too much.

This should probably be more than a favor a friend does, although it is also a favor. It should be something they at least enjoy doing for its own sake of reading. And if a friend ends up not wanting to do this, that's just fine too and worth accepting. Friends aren't friends for everything. Just like a good friend of mine for years can also not necessarily like the way I drive.

It can be tough to put a good group of beta readers together at first. This tends to get easier as you continue writing and find more people who like your work.

If you are also seeking beta readers to leave reviews on commercial sites like Amazon, I heartily recommend you get links from prospective beta readers to some of their previous reviews. You don't need or even want universally glowing and uncritical reviews. You do want to screen out unreasonable and negative trolls who will take stars off your book like it's their hobby. Which it just might be. You'll thank me.

SIDE NOTE: **external human editors**

If and when you can, get your book edited by someone else. Find a respected editor who is experienced in your g genre. Even if you only do this once, that edit from a good editor will teach you so much about what you want to write. But really, every book should get edited. There's a reason why almost every single successful author has had an editor. They *work*.

. . .

ON A RELATED NOTE: **If you're stuck and not moving forward, stop editing**

If you are having trouble completing a short story or novel, and/or if you have not yet finished a story and find yourself instead of spending time working on prior sections:

Stop editing. Just write the next page. At most drop some notes in comments for a *later* revision pass. If you see something that's egregious and quick to fix, that can be fine. But if that's starting to impede your forward motion, skip it and move on.

To repeat the importance of completing, from another angle: a first draft is often a good place to just try a bunch of things out and see how they work. Reaching the ending itself can provide great information and insight into what works.

Many times we can work and shape and draft and perfect entire scenes earlier in the book, and then have a much harder time just letting them go if it ends up the ending doesn't need them at all. Or even worse, we can find that the parts we've put so much effort into are working against the ending.

A relieving note is that with modern publishing, these darlings don't have to entirely disappear. They can become fun alternate takes for readers, and can be worked into separate short stories that take place in the same universe.

GENERAL PRINCIPLES **I've found useful in writing and reviewing**

10% rule

Proposed by Stephen King in his book "On Writing", this is quite simple. When you think you're done with a draft, go through it again and find a way to remove 10% of the total words.

I have tried this, and have found that I invariably find ways to boil down what I thought was done and make it better. Author Ken Rand goes a bit further with specific suggestions that are often fruitful, such as searching for "of". It often occurs in passive phrases that can be made both shorter and more direct, such as "day of the week" instead of "day."

. . .

The First Five *Pages*

This concept comes from the book The First Five Pages. I've found it so useful. The basic concept: make the first five pages sing. Make the first page sing. Then make the first paragraph sing. Then, after that, make the first two sentences grip.

Which brings us to the power of beginnings.

Beginnings: *the Beginning*

One of the last things you can do to help a book once everything else is in place, is work on its beginning.

There are many excellent books that cover writing beginnings, such as Beginnings, Middles and Endings by Writer's Digest. In addition to reading books on that part of craft directly, you can acquaint yourself with the power of beginnings from looking at anthologies. Pick up any short story anthology in your preferred genre that has a bunch of acknowledged masters in it, that also has a large number of stories you haven't already read. Go through it and highlight the first two sentences of every story, and then move on to the next. Do this whether it's in print, Kindle, or some other form.

Now go back and look at those sentences, and compare them to each other. Which ones work? How well do they work? It's just amazing how much information, feeling and expectation can be crammed into just a couple of sentences. Like the seed the whole tree grows from, to grow and turn in its own ways that are both surprising and, once they've branched, inevitable.

I did this with the fantasy anthology Songs of the Dying Earth, and found the results more instructive than I expected. It's one thing to consider this intellectually, and it's another thing to experience it in so many different writers' individual styles.

As is interesting but perhaps not surprising, my favorite two-sentence beginning came from master writer George R. R. Martin. Mark my words, that kid's going to make it big someday.

You can perform a similar exercise in any bookstore or library, as well as online where many bestselling books have free excerpts of opening chapters. Pick a bestseller section and check the first two sentences of every book in a row.

To repeat what I said at the start, this is a good *last* step. Once you have the story in place how you want it, with the ending that you want, is a fine time to start putting the final touches on the beginning.

And if you happen to have started with a great couple of sentences, that's fine too. There is never any obligation to rewrite what may already be working great.

A LAST WORD on rewriting

Rewriting can be difficult emotionally as well as intellectually. If you happen not to feel some emotional pain while rewriting a work, fantastic! I sincerely salute you.

Otherwise, as stated earlier but bears repeating, feeling down during a rewrite is completely natural. In fact, *it is often an expected part of the process.*

So don't feel down on yourself for possibly feeling down. Art can be tough. You are doing a tough thing that's worth doing because you want to do it. You got this.

9. **TOOLS**

As a rule, I'm a big fan of software that's available on as many platforms as possible. The best usually are (with the rare example of Vellum and similar niche fantastically well-done tools).

I'm also very much not a fan of subscription software. There might be some times where it's not avoidable – but that's very rare.

PROJECT MANAGEMENT

Trello

Make and keep lists of tasks that you can check off, organize, and share with collaborators. Available as a website, and also for Android and Apple smartphones and tablets. Trello.com

Workflowy

A site to help track and cross off tasks. Workflowy is free if you add less than 250 items a month. It's less featured than Trello, and also endearingly far simpler. It is literally and only a way to make lists that you can easily update, indent, outdent, and tag.

Writer Matthew Wayne Selznick has his own process which uses Workflowy here:

https://www.mattselznick.com/workflowy-free-outliner-writing-app/

Pomodoro timers –

This is a simple Pomodoro timer and tracker, somewhat aptly named <u>Sympl Productivity</u>. A similar app for the iPhone is <u>Be Focused</u>.

NOTE-TAKING and digital journaling

Rocketbook

An excellent reusable notebook that partners with an app you can put on your phone. Good for visual art, lyrics, stories, you name it. You can back up anything made here to the cloud and then erase the page you wrote. This effectively means an infinite-paged notebook with pages you can access from anywhere.

Evernote

EverNote is a well-established app that's available on all plat-forms. Some people love it and swear by it. I say try it. For me I like things much simpler than EverNote offers. I don't want to pick what kind of note I want to make, where to save it, etc. I just want to hit a button and start talking or writing.

OneNote

Also available on all platforms, this offering from Microsoft that actually works fine for me, OneNote is great for note-taking and note-reviewing on the run.

Email

We can also just email ourselves notes! Almost all of you reading this have a smartphone of some sort. Emailed notes can become an easily reachable, searchable and riff-able store of ideas.

I use Gmail as my main email client, and have a filter set up so that anything I email myself that has "Story Idea" in the subject line is assigned a label to that effect. Then when I want to check out story ideas I have a quick way to look them up.

Kanka.io, Notebook.ai and WorldAnvil

The website Kanka.io site is a useful way to build out worlds before writing in them. This way I can put my notions into a clear structure, and continue adding to them while I write the story so I can fill out a clear and consistent world.

If this site is not your cup of worlds, Notebook.ai offers a free alternative. Other writers I know have quite enjoyed WorldAnvil, which does require a subscription of $3-10 a month depending on the features.

Scrivener

Scrivener is all-around great writing software, as well as note-taking software. It was originally developed to help one particular writer's desire to fly through a first draft as easily as possible. It now suits that as well as many other things. One of the most fully-featured writing programs on the market, as well as one of the cheapest--as of this writing the desktop version comes in at $49. Available on all platforms except Android, which is hopefully in the works.

Graphics

Artists of many different fields end up needing to use graphics programs at one point or another, and writers are no exception. I use a version of Adobe Photoshop that's from before they switched to a subscription model – my needs haven't changed much there for many years.

A quite powerful and free alternative to Photoshop is Gimp. Similarly strong and quite inexpensive is Affinity Photo. Finally, Photoshop Elements is still non-subscription and relatively cheap at $69 as of this writing.

Some other alternatives that can be even cheaper and offer available stock photos include Canva and Bookbrush. They're quite popular for creating graphic ads and other digital media those creating can create to help other people find out about their creations.

For file storage, as long as the file is some sort of .jpg you can probably store it for free on Google Photos. If you already have Amazon Prime, you can also store an unlimited amount of jpegs on Amazon Photos.

If you take photos for a lot of people and want some more features with unlimited storage, SmugMug offers pretty good value with a basic plan of $5.99/mo or $48/yr. This includes creating albums with passwords and offering people direct connections to buy prints.

MUSIC

I like making music, so I thought it would be good to drop some cheap and pro-quality music-making software here also.

Reaper

Reaper is a fully featured digital audio workstation with live recording, midi orchestration and other features for the pretty hard to beat price of: free.

Don't be misled by the price. I know artists who have completed and released albums of high quality, both in audio and in creativity, with this software. It's available for both Mac and PC platforms and has an experimental version for Linux.

Audacity

Another great example of creators helping creators, this audio editing program is both excellent and free. In some ways it is superior to paid programs that I know of. This is especially the case with some very specifically developed plugins to help create audiobooks with professional quality sound. This can be especially important if and when uploading books to outlets like Audible. Audacity is fully available on Mac, PC and Linux.

MuseScore

If you'd like to create music in standard notation, here's a great program to just that. Also available on Mac, PC and Linux.

FILE BACKUP

Back up what you're working on! There's no longer any need to be worried about computer crashes for any reason. Once you've set it up, it doesn't even require effort. You can have your files easily synced to the cloud and never be at the mercy of losing your most recent creative work ever again.

Dropbox, Microsoft's Box, Google Drive and Apple's iCloud all offer up to several gigabytes of storage free. They're all multi-platform. If you haven't started using one of them or a similar cloud service to back up your writing, you should stop reading this book and do that right now. When your computer goes down or you switch to a new one and forget some files, you will be very thankful that you did.

DICTATION

For increased wordcount and ease of first drafting, dictation software can be *extremely* useful. When I first started using dictation it almost *doubled* my first draft word count per hour. While there are possible technical challenges to getting it set up, the payoff in terms of speed and ease is well worth considering.

Dictation with Dragon

I am using Dragon by Nuance. Unfortunately for future Apple users, it was recently discontinued for the Mac. But it is available with full support for PC. There are subscription-based Dragon apps for iPhone and Android also. (Skip further down for more recommendations for other platforms.)

I've used Dragon for live transcription, and also to transcribe voice notes I've recorded separately when I've been away from my computer. When I was driving a lot for a particular job I dictated a lot of text this way--recording the note, and then uploading the recorded .wav file to the Dragon app later.

I do recommend training it for your individual voice, headset and speech habits -- a lot of people skip this step and don't get as good results. It should take no more than half an hour or so. (I also wonder if this process is where someone at DreamWorks came up with the title for "How To Train Your Dragon.)

A flip side of using dictation is that where will always be some transcription mistakes. Usually no more than one or two errors per paragraph. That is enough to require a quick review, which can end up giving me the added bonus of cleaner first-draft copy. I'll always go beyond fixing simple transcription errors and clean up adverbs, add in further details, sharpen turns of phrase etc.

You can also watch the text as it's added and pause to fix such errors on the fly, which is also useful.

I use the Corsair Void Pro Gaming headset for dictation and I've found it perfect for my needs. I also expect just about any gaming headset will work great. They're specifically designed so gamers can coordinate how they're slaying fantastic beasts. Turns out it works just as well for dictating stories about fantastic beasts.

A side benefit of using dictation is that you can now refer to yourself as a dictator. The amount you want to be a power hungry dictator is up to you.

Dictation on Macs

For the Mac, iOS has full support of speech to text with a lot of similar options that Dragon had. It might require some setup for your system. More information and steps here.

You can also transcribe audio for free from your iOS phone with Transcribe. EverNote also has a transcription option for audio files, which is reportedly supplied by Google Voice.

- When writing a first draft, especially early in your writing career, it's very important to write to the finish.
- There are many different ways you can almost certainly increase your word count per hour.
- Rewriting is tough and worth doing, all authors in history do it.
- Critiques groups can be helpful in getting feedback on what you've written. It also is worthwhile to separate useful feedback from what isn't, and to make sure you don't stay in any situation where you are being made to feel small or less than in any way.

And that's all for now, folks! Go forth and create!

Create whatever you want, as much as possible! And keep increasing what's possible.

The preceding pages contain many of the methods I've assembled to help me create while holding down a day job. A day job which I still have.

I am always learning more, because I always want to grow.

Growth is another thing I love about creating. Besides the gifts that creating brings me, such as new stories, or songs, or pictures, creating helps me advances myself. It not only brings the new into my life, it brings a new me to me.

So I encourage you to grow. Continue to try what you've found in here, and anything else you find. No matter what, to repeat what I've hoped to make clear throughout this book in many ways: be kind to yourself.

Below you'll find another certificate and permission slip that you've well earned, and long before you ever checked out this book.

Thanks for coming along on this trip with me! And again, as always, please feel free to take what's useful, revamp it in any way that suits you, and junk the rest. It's all about what works, and what *plays*.

CERTIFICATES

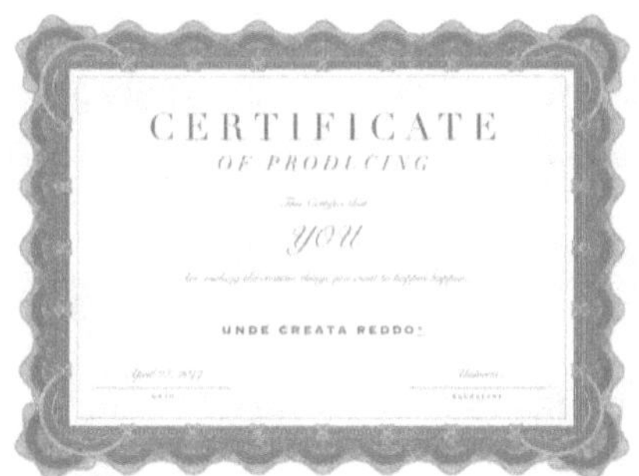

Permission Slip

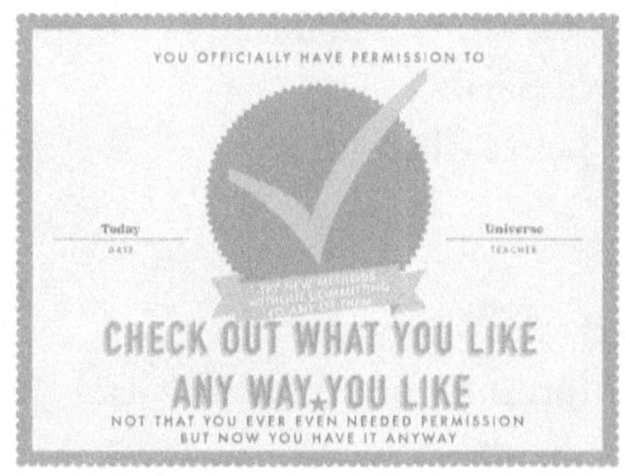

FURTHER RESOURCES

Certificates
All of the certificates in this book are freely available here:
Creating With a Day Job: Certificates

Books
Here are some books I've found very useful.

Motivation and outlook
The Miracle Morning - Hal Elrod
The War of Art - Steven Pressfield
Art & Fear - David Bayles
Atomic Habits - James Clear

Motivation for writers
The Miracle Morning for Writers - Hal Elrod, Steve Scott, Honoree Corder, S.J. Scott
Becoming a Writer - Dorothea Brande
On Writing - Stephen King

Bird by Bird - Anne Lamott
One Continuous Mistake - Gail Sher

WRITING Craft
Booklife: Strategies and Survival Tips for the 21st Century Writer - Jeff VanderMeer
No Plot, No Problem - Jeff Baty
2K to 10K - Rachel Aaron
5,000 Words Per Hour - Chris Fox
Story - Robert McKee
The Writer's Guide to Training Your Dragon - Scott Baker
Story Flash by Alexander Astremsky.
The First Five Pages by Noah Lukeman
Beginnings, Middles and Endings by Writer's Digest
Characters by Writer's Digest
$30 Writing School by Michael W. Dean

OTHER CREATIVE FIELDS
$30 Music School and $30 Film School, also by Michael W. Dean. The cover for Film School looks janky but the info is solid.
Podcasts
If you enjoy podcasts from your smartphone, I can recommend these apps below. There are many other apps, and also you can usually listen to podcasts via your smartphone's web browser.

Podcasts
Mobile apps
DoggCatcher - Android
Stitcher - iOs, Android

WRITING podcasts

- General inspiration
- Happier by Gretchen Rubin. Practicing happiness in daily life.
- The Moment with Brian Koppelman. Discussions with creative people about their creative processes.
- WTF with Marc Maron. While not necessarily everyone's cup of tea, Marc Maron offers consistently excellent interviews with top creative artists of many different fields.
- Writing
- Writing Excuses
- Speculate!
- The Write Life
- A Way With Words (NPR)
- Dead Robots Society
- Helping Writers Become Authors
- Music
- Meet the Composer. Direct interviews with modern classical composers.
- Song Exploder. Deep dives into what makes modern music work.
- Everything Music with Rick Beato (YouTube). Rick Beato has an excellent way of diving deep into well-known popular music and showing us the nuts and bolts that put them together. His videos range from guitar fingerpicking patterns to film scoring to pragmatically useful overviews of music theory.

VISUAL ART PODCASTS

- Raw Material. Direct from the San Francisco Museum of Modern Art (SFMOMA), this explores modern and contemporary art through direct interviews with artists.

- Bad at Sports. This wryly titled podcast has direct interviews with current artists.
- Dr Janina Ramirez - Art Detective. Art history and discussion with current art experts.
- The Artsy Podcast. A wide overview of how art is happening in modern culture.
- A Golden Age of Art Podcasts. A good overview of these and other podcasts related to the field of visual art.

WEB RESOURCES

Habits and process

How to Build a New Habit: Your Strategy Guide

Does Having a Day Job Mean Making Better Art?

How I Learned to be an Optimist in a Week

How to Stop Overthinking

The Mystery of Picasso - Done in 1956, this film follows Picasso painting new works in real time. Above is a link to the Amazon Prime streaming version.

MARATHONS

National Novel Writing Month

The RPM Challenge

30 Paintings in 30 Days

Daily Design Challenges

WRITING

Dan Harmon's Story Circle - A web link to a free article. This method has saved me so many hours of time.

How to Write a Mystery - A lot of good things to consider here. As always, your mileage may vary so take only what helps you.

Lester Dent's Pulp Fiction Rules - You mileage may vary quite a bit here also. That said, I heartily suggest giving writing this way a shot just to see what might shake loose for you.

Worldbuilding Master List - from the very useful area of Reddit.com known as r/worldbuilding, here's a compilation of resources for the creation of fictional worlds.

Worldbuilding 101 - A master of worldbuilding takes you through a very well structured process that can be a structure for creativity and story. Your possibly galactice or even universal mileage may vary.

How to Give Useful Critiques - Hugo and Nebula award-winning author Mary Robinette Kowal's admirably succinct set of charts on using critiques to get the information you need.

CLOSING QUOTE

A closing quote

I like to relate to many different creators across many different fields. Here is a link to master actor Robert Forster, speaking on excellence. The whole piece is well worth reading. I would like to zero in on this chunk of wisdom in particular.

> ....life is a series of moments along this arc, moments at which you can deliver excellence, or less, if you desire. But if you do deliver excellence...You get the reward of self-respect and respect from others and satisfaction. And this is the real McCoy. This is untransferrable wealth. You stick this in your pocket and it's like a little nugget; it'll always be there.
>
> ... Those in both religious traditions, the Eastern and the Western, talk about a path: the path of righteousness.
>
> ....But if you're one of the ones who believe that inner peace is the best life has to offer, you know precisely what you're doing when you wake up in the morning. You're using your life and your life experiences to understand with, and with every action you create, you deliver that understanding. You're doing what an artist does: using his life to understand and deliver that understanding with

every act you create. And if you're doing that, and you're getting those rewards on a frequent enough basis, you're making the best that you can out of the life you've got to live.

NOTES

ACKNOWLEDGMENTS

A book like this is the accumulation of a lot of useful information. I can sincerely thank every single person I've ever talked with or who's book I ever read, whether I agreed or disagreed. Some books I found most helpful are cited, with my unending gratitude to their thoughtful and generous authors.

For this particular book I also specifically thank EY. Their full name is hidden out of respect for their privacy, but their relentless stand for kindness and compassion has inspired me greatly in all aspects of my life.

I also thank my favorite writer's group of all time, and in particular the feedback of Alan Peterson, Deb McIntyre who had the great idea of creating permission slips and certificates. Many other inspiring people also helped, and I am flattered to have benefited from their great thoughts.

I also thank the usual gang of personal angels who have given me clear feedback from the best kind of kindness: wanting to help me be even more clear and better. It's hard to see one's own forest of words, I thank them as great surveyors as well as great friends.

I thank you, whether or not you agree with anything I have to say, for being interested in creativity and in creating. I hope you will treat yourself with the kindness and compassion you deserve just for being you.

And finally I thank creativity itself, as one of the most beautiful things I know of in a universe of surpassing beauty. I say "surpassing" with specific intent: the universe is infinitely beautiful, and manages the great trick of being ever more beautiful than is possible, forever alerting us to entirely new realities of beauty.

I love all of you in this journey through humanity, the universe and beyond.

ABOUT THE AUTHOR

James Beach is a writer, photographer and recovering musician. He has worked a wide variety of day jobs including fast food fry station manager, industrial roofer, home cleaner and information technology professional for Fortune 500 companies.

While working at these and other day jobs he has written several novels and multiple screen plays, performed with several different bands, composed soundtracks for stage and film, voice acted and directed animation pilots, performed standup comedy, recorded and released music albums ranging from electronica to progressive metal, and cooked for himself without starving.

He was born and raised in New Jersey, and was once told he was a bad Photoshop superimposition on the East Coast. He successfully escaped and now lives in San Francisco, a perfect locale for exploring his emerging super powers.

For more declassified information, visit
jimbeach.net